FOREIGN POLICY AND THE FREE SOCIETY

WALTER MILLIS

JOHN COURTNEY MURRAY, S.J.

Foreign Policy and the Free Society

The Discussants:

A. A. BERLE, JR.

SCOTT BUCHANAN

EUGENE BURDICK

ERIC F. GOLDMAN

ROBERT M. HUTCHINS

CLARK KERR

HENRY R. LUCE

REINHOLD NIEBUHR

ROBERT REDFIELD

Published for The Fund for the Republic by Oceana Publications

Contents

The Contributors to This Book

WALTER MILLIS is a military historian and journalist, the author of such books as *The Martial Spirit, Road to War, This Is Pearl!* and *Arms and Men,* and the editor of *The Forrestal Diaries.* He is staff administrator of the project on the Common Defense, one of the studies within the Fund for the Republic's basic issues program.

JOHN COURTNEY MURRAY, S.J., one of the Consultants on the Basic Issues to the Fund for the Republic, is professor of theology at Woodstock College, Maryland, and editor of *Theological Studies.* He has written extensively on both theological and secular matters.

A. A. BERLE, JR. is an attorney, former Assistant Secretary of State, and author of *The Modern Corporation and Private Property* (with Gardiner C. Means) and *The 20th Century Capitalist Revolution,* among other books.

SCOTT BUCHANAN, philosopher and author, has taught at several universities, and was Dean of St. John's College from 1937 to 1947. *Essay in Politics* is his most recent book.

EUGENE BURDICK is a professor of political science at the University of California at Berkeley and the author of the popular novel on American politics, *The Ninth Wave.*

ERIC F. GOLDMAN is professor of history at Princeton University. He was awarded the Bancroft Prize for distinguished American history in 1952 for his book, *Rendezvous With Destiny,* a history of modern American reform. He has also written *The Crucial Decade, America, 1945-55.*

ROBERT M. HUTCHINS, President of the Fund for the Republic, serves as Chairman of the Consultants on the Basic Issues. He is former President and Chancellor of the University of Chicago.

CLARK KERR is President of the University of California and a specialist in labor economics. He has served as arbitrator in many labor-management negotiations.

HENRY R. LUCE is the founder of the magazines, *Time, Life, Fortune,* and *Sports Illustrated,* and editor-in-chief of these as well as of *Architectural Forum* and *House and Home.*

REINHOLD NIEBUHR is Vice President of the Union Theological Seminary and graduate professor of applied Christianity. He is the author of many books, most recently *Pious and Secular America.*

ROBERT REDFIELD, professor of anthropology at the University of Chicago since 1927, is a past President of the American Anthropological Association and the author of *Peasant Society and Culture, The Primitive World and Its Transformations, A Village That Chose Progress.*

Foreword

IN THEIR SEARCH to determine what a free society is and
how it may be maintained in twentieth century America,
the Consultants on the Basic Issues to the Fund for the Republic determined that it was necessary for them to examine,
among other things, the consequences for liberty of the
foreign and military policies of the United States. Four
meetings of the Consultants during the winter and spring
of 1957-58 were devoted to this question. Out of these
meetings grew the papers presented in this book by Walter
Millis and John Courtney Murray. The book also includes a
highly abridged version of the Consultants' "conversations."

All of the Consultants participated in the discussion and
all are represented in this abridgment except Dr. I. I. Rabi,
who felt that his position as a member of the President's
Science Advisory Committee forbade placing his views on
the public record.

The papers and the discussion make no attempt at
definitive answers to the extremely complicated questions
involved in the foreign and military policies of this country
in their relation to the character, standards, and goals of the
free society. There are, in fact, disagreements on many
points, consensus on a few, and no conclusions. However,
we believe that the material herein is worth presenting as—
to quote Father Murray's words on the final page of this
book—"a contribution to public understanding."

ROBERT M. HUTCHINS

By Walter Millis

THE UNITED STATES is now entangled in courses of military and foreign policy which appear to tend only toward eventual catastrophe. With the Soviet Union, it is committed to a nuclear weapons race of almost inconceivable deadliness, of which a probable ultimate outcome is an intercontinental war of mass extermination in which the American as well as the Soviet system would certainly perish, and perhaps civilization with them. In the meanwhile, under the enormous material and moral costs of this arms race we must expect a steady erosion of the personal and political liberties traditional in our free society; while to live under the shadow of doom at home brings no compensatory strength to our foreign policies. An indefinite continuation of this state of affairs threatens only a deterioration of American, as opposed to Soviet, influence over the development of world history.

I believe that less calamitous courses must and can be found. Current debate is already indicating the directions in which solutions may lie. But if they are to be found, I believe that the United States as well as the Soviet Union must make a more positive contribution than either has yet offered toward the discovery.

The cold war was not of American making, yet Americans should realize that they have, by their official policies and the public attitudes which dictate official policy, been unable to moderate its tension, to diminish the difficulties of even minor clarification, or to decrease the tempo of the nuclear-missile competition.

Americans have generally accepted a concept of the world problem—repeatedly set forth in the speeches of our statesmen and arguments of our publicists—which finds a forceful and official restatement in the "Declaration of Principles" by the NATO Conference in Paris in December 1957:

> The free world faces the mounting challenge of international communism backed by Soviet power. Only last month in Moscow the Communist rulers again gave clear warning of their determination to press on to domination over the entire world, if possible by subversion, if necessary by violence . . . For the entire world it is both a tragedy and a great danger that the peoples under international Communist rule—their national independence, human liberties and their standard of living as well as their scientific and technological achievements —have been sacrificed to the purposes of world domination and military power. The suppression of their liberty will not last forever.

In accordance with this concept of the world problem Americans have assumed that the greatest peril confronting their society is that of military attack, which the Soviet Union may launch upon us (or upon our allies) the moment it has acquired the military ability to do so without exposing itself to catastrophic reprisal. To make the reprisal certain we have ringed the Soviet Union with military air bases armed with thermo-nuclear bombs, thereby stimulating the Soviet Union to develop intermediate-range ballistic missiles intended to "take out" the bases before reprisal can descend— to which in turn we are forced to make reply.

This concept has done nothing to discourage its mirror image, sedulously propagated by the Russians, that "Western capitalism" is the force which is sacrificing all peoples to "the purposes of world domination and military power." It adds to the difficulties of rational negotiation with the Russians; it fortifies their intense suspicions of our purposes while so enflaming Western suspicion and distrust that productive discussion of the problems which are in fact common to both the super-power systems becomes virtually impossible.

Yet the statement in the NATO "Declaration" is clearly inadequate as a description of the existing relations between the United States and the Soviet Union and of the power factors that determine them. It is even more faulty as a guide to policy. It is true that in forty years Communist governance has spread from control over no more than a meeting-hall in Petrograd to control over about one-third of the population of the globe. But to regard this astonishing development—to which many historical forces contributed and which followed many different patterns in different areas—simply as the result of a conspiracy by something called "international communism" to achieve "domination over the entire world, if possible by subversion, if not by violence," is to deny many of the most obvious facts of the past forty years. It is also to blind ourselves to the real weaknesses (which we never seem able to exploit) and the real strengths (which we seem always to overlook until it is too late) of the Russian political-imperial structure and the Communist ideological system.

I believe that better analyses of the existing world problem can be made. I believe that there are many forces at work today besides those of military terrorism. To appreciate and apply these forces properly will not solve every issue; and one can see no present possibility of any great "summit" act of peace that will answer all questions and finally avert the dreadful perils that modern society has created for itself. But many factors now clear in the international complex can be grasped and used to relax the tensions under which we are living, to reduce the tempo of the nuclear arms race to a point at which it may ultimately become manageable, to establish the bases of that "competitive co-existence" to which the two super-powers appear to be sentenced as the only alternative to a "competitive co-extinction."

Three propositions would probably be accepted today by most Americans:

That neither of the super-powers can today destroy the other, or even impose crippling restrictions on the other's freedom of action, without itself being blown to fragments in the process;

That serious conflicts between them must therefore be resolved by some process of accommodation or negotiation;

That fruitful negotiation is all but impossible in an atmosphere of war psychosis, enflamed by exaggerated suspicions and unnecessary fears.

These propositions imply no approval of Soviet aims. They merely reflect the factual situation. It is evident that this situation is leading to increasing, if less complete, agreement among Americans to some further propositions:

One: That the dangers to this country of a sudden Soviet sneak attack have been exaggerated out of all relation to reality. Secretary Dulles has expressed the conviction that the Soviet leaders not only do not want war but do not want the two nations "to drift so far apart that there is increased danger" of war. Russian memories of their 15 million dead in the Second World War are not yet two decades old; and under present conditions, which Soviet leadership seems to find satisfactory, so far as we can see, there is nothing which the Soviet Union could possibly gain by a nuclear attack on the United States even remotely commensurate with the risk it would run, even if Soviet ability to forestall reprisal were far greater than it is.

Two: That communism, both within the Soviet Union and in the Communist-controlled countries with which it has surrounded itself, is not an ephemeral system. The hope, entertained under the original "containment" policy promulgated by George F. Kennan, that if the external pressure were kept up the Communist system would dissolve itself into something else, has been abandoned by Kennan himself and most others. In confronting the Russian super-power, the United States is dealing with the effects of an enduring social revolution. It is an historic fact, as irreversible as were the French or the American revolutions; and it has produced a political-social-economic organization of society which, whether it is good or evil, has demonstrated that it is both viable and powerful.

Three: That its powers, however great, are at the same time not unlimited. Soviet Russia, like the United States, is restrained—or "deterred"—by its own fears of war. It has been unable to enforce its own solution for the German problem, just as the West has been. It felt obliged to retreat from Iran in the early post-war years, and has finally retreated from Austria. Whatever hopes it may have entertained of world conquest through subversion have suffered a severe discount. It is now obvious that American domestic communism no longer represents any significant threat to the American system or to Western policy whatever. In France and Italy, where Communist parties have enlisted substantial fractions of the electorate, Russian imperial infiltration may find greater opportunities. Yet whatever their successes, it is obvious that they could not repeat past patterns which, whether in China or in Central Europe, were overwhelmingly determined by the military-political circumstances of the Second World War. While Russian maneuvers and infiltrations in the Arab or Southeast Asian worlds present difficulties and dangers to Western statesmanship, it is unrealistic to regard them as simply extensions of past Communist expansions, which themselves differed greatly one from another, and all of which were shaped by conditions that do not now exist.

Russian military power—while beyond challenge in dealing with internal revolt, as Hungary clearly demonstrated—has not since 1945 been effectively exerted beyond the frontiers then attained. (The conquests of China and North Vietnam were not, in either origin or conduct, primarily Russian enterprises.) The Russian Communist power system has tenaciously and successfully defended every power position achieved in 1945. It has matched the United States in the weapons of threat and terror. It has called up, in China, a potentially great ally, much as the United States has called up the Grand Alliance of NATO. But beyond this it has not been able to go; and it is at least conceivable that it has already arrived at the practicable limits of its reach.

From these propositions it should be possible, it seems, to construct a different and more useful picture of international society than that of an inappeasable "war," waged between a West cowering upon a military and psychological defensive against an imperial Russia, bent remorselessly upon a military domination of the world. But the task is not easy. Among those in the West who accept these common-sense propositions, and to whom the cruder follies of the war psychology— as well as the appalling dangers which they carry with them —are apparent, there remains a deep division. To one group, represented by figures like George F. Kennan in the United States, Aneurin Bevan (in some of his moods) in Britain, Ollenhauer and the Socialists in West Germany, the true international picture has become one in which peace is at least possible. Or if not peace, at least a degree of accommodation, adjustment, detente, or *modus vivendi* which will reduce the threat of nuclear extermination to a point where it may become more rationally manageable.

To the other broad group, of which Secretary Dulles and the President are outstanding examples, peace is not possible. This statement requires explanation. Holders of this view grant at once that the last thing which the Soviet Union wants is an intercontinental megaton war; that it will accept considerable risks to its local interests in order to avoid one; and that even in local situations it is unlikely to employ military power to advance its foreign policies, since other and better means are usually available to it. In this view, the intercontinental war is not, except as it may be set off by accident, any great present risk. It may even be admitted that the basic aggressive drives commonly attributed to the Soviet system are less powerful, more subject to the corrections of time and circumstances, than is usually supposed. But in this view, the Russian Communist system remains fundamentally and inappeasably aggressive. It is an empire of immense power, driven and directed by a dogmatic concept of world history which, while demonstrably false, is believed by those who control its destinies, and believed by them the more sincerely because their own survival depends upon the belief. This dogma not only compels them implacably to threaten the non-Communist world; even worse, it renders it impossible for them to make a peace with the non-Communist world.

Secretary Dulles—who is always beseeching the Russians to make peace—does not put it so bluntly. But at the core of this view is the belief that the Soviet Union not only does not want to but in a real sense cannot make peace with the West on terms compatible with Western survival. It cannot accept free elections in East Germany, because the idea of free elections—obviously poisonous to any totalitarian system—would spread back through the satellites into the heart of the Soviet empire. It cannot accept genuine inspection of armaments because this would destroy too much of the secrecy essential to the succesful operation of the police state. It cannot come to the appearance, even, of a peaceful settlement with the West because this would destroy the spectre of capitalistic encroachment and invasion which is essential to the regime to maintain its hold over its own people.

In this view, consequently, the Soviet Union is not only implacably aggressive but cannot, by its very nature, be otherwise. One cannot make peace with an organism which by its nature is incapable of making peace. The only alternative is to contain it indefinitely until, by the gradual operation of historic forces of one kind or another, it is transformed into a kind of organism which is capable of making peace with an essentially unchanged Western society. There is, it may be said, much that is persuasive in this view. It seemed quite adequate when it was first stated in its essentials by Kennan in his famous "containment" article in *Foreign Affairs* in 1947.

But the tensions of today (reflected in Kennan's own subsequent change of viewpoint) arise precisely because it seems increasingly inadequate to conditions as they have developed. The Russian Communist power system, while it has undergone certain superficial modification, has shown no signs whatever of those fundamental transformations necessary (in this view) to make peace again a possibility. In the political, psychological, and economic spheres, at least, containment seems not to be containing. The Western power system as a whole is not remaining unchanged; it may be undergoing transformation even more rapidly than the Russian Communist power system. Finally, this view of the world situation has found no answer for the frightful intensification of the military problem, which is generally believed to be the most dangerous of all confronting us.

The military foundations of containment rest upon the continuance of a balance, or equality, of retaliatory terror. The United States and the Soviet Union already probably possess armaments sufficiently dreadful and deliverable to establish this equality of deterrence. But military balances are inherently unstable. The effort, by both sides, to make sure of its deterrent has generated the absolutely insane race in weapons of greater terror and more perfect deliverability— a race which brings nearer every day the possibility that it will of itself break down by accident or misunderstanding into a catastrophic destruction of civilization. In the meanwhile, it serves only to paralyze the more normal use of military force in the play of international relations. This is in turn eroding the whole structure of the American alliance system, which from NATO through SEATO to the Far Eastern Alliance, is founded upon the concept of conventional military action. It does not, unfortunately, have any corresponding effect upon the Soviet alliance system, which, while not without its military aspects, is founded basically on political and ideological factors.

Here is the greatest dilemma of what might be called the "containment" or "no peace" approach. Some rather desperate attempts have been made to escape it by somehow bringing war back into the international scene as a usable instrument of policy. The argument is that we can still continue to contain the Soviet Union by making war, but we must make only "limited" war in the process. This, however, requires the further argument that if the West carefully confines itself to limited war it can trust the Soviet Union to do likewise. For a nation which spends so much of its breath proclaiming that "you can't trust the Russians" this simply leads to an impasse. Aside from all the technical difficulties involved in keeping a war waged with "tactical" atomic weapons limited in its scope and terror, the concept of limited war presents a simple fallacy in logic. Obviously, limited war is possible only for objectives which are not of vital importance to the survival of either contestant. Therefore, we can resort to it only when the objective is not vital to either side—in which case we would be unlikely to resort to war in any event, as happened in Indo-China, Suez, Hungary—while *limited* war is no more a protection than the super-giant bombs against those Soviet aggressions which we believe really are vital to our own survival.

This dilemma has not been resolved by the no-peace school, and cannot be resolved by any number of repeated appeals to the Russians to disarm, to allow free elections, to submit to a United Nations authority loaded against them, or to make peace on any other of the terms which the West has so often advanced in the name of "peace" and which, by this very analysis, can only amount to defeat. If the Russian government is by its nature incapable of making peace, then to offer it peace is in fact simply to demand that it surrender.

Admittedly, the opposite school is not free from dilemmas of its own. In this view, it is unrealistic to assume that the Russian dictatorship is remorselessly driven by a false but self-consistent ideology and dogma, clearly predictable in its consequences. Moscow, hardly less frequently than Washington, appears to depart in practice from the canon and apocrypha of the official faith. Like Washington or London, its policies appear to respond much more to the fears or opportunities of the moment than to long-range calculation of means to world domination. Instincts of self-defense are certainly as prominent in its actions as those of aggression. The Russian problem is in fact very much like our own; both the great power systems are in what is really a common predicament. They are in clear conflict; yet neither believes that the conflict can be resolved by the military destruction of the other. In each power there are "adventurists" (the Russian phrase) or "advocates of preventive war" (as we call them), but there is only the remotest chance that such men will take control of the policy of either.

There seems to have emerged a kind of tacit agreement between the two super-powers more significant than the issues which divide them. They are in agreement in that neither wants war. They are agreed in that neither wants nor intends to force issues to the ultimate. Each realizes that the missile-megaton arms race, now only in its early stages, must break them both if carried to its logical conclusions. Working from such a foundation as this, it should be possible to arrive at a detente in those areas—primarily Germany, the Middle East, and perhaps Southeast Asia— where interests of the two come most directly and significantly into contact.

Since the fundamental fact of the contemporary international system is the existence of the two mutually deterrent nuclear arsenals, these presumably must be maintained. But if it is impossible to put an end to the armaments, it might be practicable at least to end the arms race. Since it is the *balance* of terror which sustains the existing peace, each power system might be brought to agree not to attempt to upset it by further competitive development of more powerful, more irresistible, and inherently more dangerous systems of mass-destruction weapons.

Such are the possibilities which those who believe that peace, or at least a significant truce, can be achieved would seek to explore. They are in the dilemma, however, that to achieve such stabilizing adjustments in the relationship each power system must accept the other and, to a large extent, take it into partnership. It is obviously out of the question to normalize relations in the Far East without full recognition of Communist China and her acceptance as a great power in her own right. It is apparent that Russia will not relinquish her power position in East Germany without some return which will make the bargain attractive to the Kremlin leaders; and it is difficult to think of any such return which the West could offer short of accepting Communist control of Central Europe and in effect becoming the Kremlin's partner in its maintenance. Churchill in the later war years was willing to contemplate a revival of the old system of "spheres of interest" in the Near East and the Balkans. Such immoral ideas were indignantly rejected by the Americans, but the possibility that something of the kind may become the price of peace cannot be denied and must be faced fairly by those whose objective is, after all, a reconciliation of the two great systems in "competitive co-existence."

They must also face the dilemma that if the co-existence must continue to be competitive, something like equal terms of competition must be worked out. They do not now exist. Industrial competitors normally operate within the same rules

—the mechanisms of price competition or competition in service or productive efficiency are open to both. In a monopolistic situation this relation no longer obtains; the rules are different for the monopolists than they are for the independents who would challenge them. The Communist power system operates on one set of rules, so to speak, the non-Communist power system on a different set, and it is almost as difficult to establish any genuine competition between them as between, say, the great American grocery chains and the remaining independent grocers. The competition between the Communist and non-Communist worlds uses certain terms common to both—just as price considerations are not wholly absent from the relations between the independent grocers and the big chains—but they are not the significant terms. This is hardly at all a military competition; it is only in small part a "competition for the minds of men"; it is only partially a competition in the ability rapidly to raise the standard of living of underdeveloped areas over the world.

It is probable that the democratic-capitalistic West is still superior in all these competitive potentialities, but even among those who most strongly assert its superiority in these respects one finds no confidence at all that it will be able to withstand the Communist challenge. Western spokesmen too often sound like a hypothetical industrialist who might say of a rival: "I can beat him on prices, on production costs, on service, on the excellence of my labor relations, on salesmanship, but he is taking my business all the same and one day will be certain to undo me." One could conclude from such a statement that there must be some hidden factor here; that the competitive situation was not fully expressed in the conventional terms; that this was not, in fact, a "competition" at all, since there can be no real competition except on mutually equal rules.

Those who hope to establish a "competitive co-existence" must still meet the problem of competitive rules. The significant competition between the Communist and non-Communist worlds is not in military power, in ideas, or in economic productivity. It is a competition between two different systems for the organization of men into that degree of submission or cooperation required by the demands of the highly integrated and highly specialized modern society. The Communist system might prove less efficient as an industrial producer and still triumph as a more efficient way of getting the organization done; the Western world might prove superior both as producer and as provider of a freer and more humane way of life, and still fail just because it could not organize the hundreds of millions uncommitted, at heart, to either system. In either case, the result would not be the outcome of a "competition," for no elements of competition would be present. It would be the outcome of the "co-existence," since it would flow from the simple fact of two different methods of organization being present on the same planet, just as the economics of the modern automotive industry flow not from the competition between the Big Three but from the fact of their co-existence.

If the no-peace party in the West has failed to solve the military dilemma, the no-war party has failed to solve the dilemma of "competitive" co-existence. To enter a partnership with the Soviet Union must tend to strengthen the Communist methods of human organization; firmly to oppose those methods and endeavor to defeat them must make partnership extraordinarily difficult. There is no clear light at the end of either avenue of approach. Those who follow one must expect to receive the frequently well-founded taunts of those who follow the other; each must expect to be told by the other that his hopes are fantastic, the risks he is running are appalling, he is imperiling the state and man's immortal soul. All one can say is that, of the two general courses, that which is willing to explore the possibilities of peace or accommodation is more hopeful than that which begins with a denial that peace is possible. The course which endeavors to examine the realities of motive and possibility in the international complex is more hopeful than that which clings to the most extreme fears of a war psychosis type and, in discounting an unknowable future, overlooks the possibilities of the actual present.

For the time being at least, the "balance of terror" appears to be operating. It has thereby created an opportunity for creative good as tremendous as its potentialities for the ultimate destruction of civilization. The continued maintenance of an effective deterrent power is a requirement for national security. It is only one. Another, no less essential to ultimate survival, is that we re-examine the actualities of the international context, that we be willing to take at least the same risks for peace that we normally take for guaranteeing victory in war, and that we use the chance which the great deterrents have provided to bring international relations into some framework in which the race toward total catastrophe can first be slowed and ultimately be ended.

By John Courtney Murray

It MAY BE A CONTRIBUTION to the present discussion if I attempt a brief statement of the unique character of the Soviet empire. Co-existence with this empire is the present fact. There are those who seek to transform the fact into a policy by adding various adjectives to the word "co-existence." There is talk, for instance, of "peaceful" co-existence, or "competitive" co-existence. But before co-existence, however adjectivally qualified, can become a policy, it is necessary to know just what kind of empire we are co-existing with.

It is not enough to cite as the single characteristic of the Soviet empire that it is intent on "world domination," and to let it go at that. The intellectual tyranny of phrases, to which we have long been accustomed in domestic politics, has invaded the field of foreign policy in consequence of the impact of democracy on the conduct of war and on the making of peace. The trouble is that the stock phrases tend to become simply incantations. They are invoked as curses on the enemy or as cries of alarm to sustain a mood of fear and opposition. So it is with the phrase "world domination." It has ceased to yield any clear demonstrable meaning. It has even acquired false connotations, as if the primary Soviet aim were domination by military conquest. In consequence some would wish to discard the phrase altogether, as unreal and unhelpful. But this would be a mistake of method that would lead to substantial error in viewing the structure of the problem that confronts America today. The phrase has meaning, but it needs to be analyzed in the light of the four unique aspects of the Soviet empire.

The Soviet Union is historically unique (1) as a state or power, (2) as an empire (*imperium*) or mode of rule, (3) as an imperialism, and (4) as the legatee of a special segment of world history.

One: Russia is unique as a state or a power. For the first time in history it has brought under a single supreme government the 210,000,000 people scattered over the 8,600,000 square miles of the Euro-Asiatic plain, the great land-mass that stretches from the River Elbe to the Pacific Ocean. This gigantic power is a police state of new proportions and unique efficiency. Within it there is no such thing as the "rule of law"; there is only the thing called "Soviet legality." Power is used according to certain forms; but there is no justice and no sense of human rights. The Soviet Union has not adopted the Western concept of law nor has it evolved a comparable concept of its own. Its theory of government is purely and simply despotism. In this respect Sir Winston Churchill was right in viewing the Russians (as Sir Isaiah Berlin reports) as a "formless, quasi-Asiatic mass beyond the walls of European civilization"; for these walls, that contain the Western realization of civility, were erected by men who understood the Western heritage of law—Roman, Greek, Germanic, Christian. The Soviet Union has no such understanding of law.

Moreover, through a novel set of institutions the Soviet Union has succeeded in centralizing all governmental power to a degree never before achieved. The ultimate organ of control is the Communist party, a small group of men who think and act under an all-embracing discipline that has likewise never before been achieved. Under its historically new system—a totally socialized economy—the Soviet Union has become an industrial and technological power whose single rival is the United States; in rising to this status of power it has chosen to emphasize industries and technologies that are related to war. This state is consequently a military power of the first order. It has no rival in ground forces; its air power is adequate to all the new exigencies of war; and for the first time in history the state that controls the Heartland of the World Island has become a sea power of a special kind, an underwater power. Finally, its nuclear capabilities, achieved in large measure independently of outside sources of information (as Deputy Secretary of Defense Quarles has recently admitted), are equal to those of the United States, for all practical purposes and many impractical ones.

Two: Russia is unique as an empire, as a manner and method of rule, as an *imperium*. It is organized and guided in accordance with a revolutionary doctrine. For the first time in history this doctrine has consciously erected an atheistic materialism into a political and legal principle that furnishes the substance of the state and determines its procedures. Soviet doctrine is exclusive and universal in its claim to furnish, not only an account of nature and history, but also a technique of historical change. It is therefore inherently aggressive in its intent; and it considers itself destined to sole survival as an organizing force in the world of politics. The Communist doctrine of the World Revolution has indeed undergone a century of change, since the days of Marx and Engels. Substantially, however, the change has been simply development. The basic inspiration has been steady and the continuity has been organic. As Prof. Albert G. Meyer has recently pointed out: "Stalinism can and must be defined as a pattern of thought and action that flows directly from

Leninism" (*Leninism*, p. 282). Prof. Bertram D. Wolfe has documented the same thesis (*Khrushchev and Stalin's Ghost*). This thesis is in possession. And there is no convincing evidence that Mr. Khrushchev represents apostasy or even heresy.

Three: Russia is unique as an imperialism. The Soviet Union is essentially an empire, not a country. Nearly half her subjects should be considered "colonial peoples." Many of the "sister republics" are no more part of Russia than India was of Great Britain. As Mr. Edward Crankshaw has reminded us, "Even if Moscow retreated to the frontiers of the Soviet Union tomorrow, Russia would still be the greatest imperial power in the world." But Mr. Crankshaw's other proposition, that "Russian imperialism is at a dead end," is by no means true. It may indeed be difficult to describe the Soviet imperial design, but this is only because it is difficult to define Soviet imperialism. It is a new historical force, not to be likened to prior mysticisms of power. It is not at all based on the concept of a master-race, or on the aggrandizement of the sacred "nation," or on the fulfillment of a noble idea, such as the rule of law to be brought to the "lesser breeds." The newness of the imperialism has almost masked the fact that it is an imperialism.

It has exhibited a new mastery of older imperialistic techniques—military conquest, the enduring threat of force, political puppetry, centralized administration of minorities, economic exploitation of "colonial" regions. It has expanded the old concept of the "ally" into the new concept of the "satellite." But perhaps its newness is chiefly revealed in the creation of the historically unique imperialistic device known as "Soviet patriotism." This is not a thing of blood and soil but of mind and spirit. It is not born of the past, its deeds and sufferings, borne in common; it looks more to the future, to the deeds yet to be done and to the sufferings still to be borne. It is a "patriotism of a higher order," and of a more universal bearing, than any of the classic feelings toward *Vaterland, la patrie,* my country. It is a loyalty to the Socialist Revolution; it is also a loyalty to the homeland of the Revolution, Russia. Its roots are many—in ideology, in economic facts, and in the love of power; in a whole cluster of human resentments and idealisms; and in the endless capacities of the human spirit for ignorance, illusion, and self-deception. This higher patriotism claims priority over all mere national loyalties. It assures to the Soviet Union a form of imperialistic penetration into other states, namely, the Fifth Column, that no government in history has hitherto commanded. Soviet imperialism, unlike former imperialisms, can be content with the creation of chaos and disorder; within any given segment of time it need not seek to impose a dominion, an order. The Soviet Union may indeed lack a finished imperial design; in any case, the concept of design is too rational for a force that owes little to reason. But it has something better for its purposes, which are inherently dark. It has a revolutionary vision.

If there must be a single phrase to sum up the intentions of Soviet imperialism, it would be far better to speak of "world revolution" than of "world domination." The word "revolution" has a definite meaning that signifies a definite possibility. The world as we know it can be radically changed; it is, in fact, changing daily before our eyes. Moreover, it is possible to know the directions of change that are implicit in the Communist world revolution, as it is guided by Communist doctrine. On the other hand, "world domination" defines not a process but a term. The term may be a Communist dream. It may even be admitted that this term is an historical possibility, if one admits that anything is possible in history. However, what we are called upon to cope with is an actuality, a process that is really going on, an intention that is presently operative—the imperialism of the World Revolution.

Four: The Soviet Union is unique as the legatee of a longer history. It is the inheritor both of Tsarist imperialism and of mystical panslavist messianism. It carries on, at the same time that it fundamentally transforms, the myth of Holy Russia, the "spiritual people," the "godbearing children of the East," whose messianic destiny is to rescue humanity from the "Promethean West." Communism, whether in theory or in practice, is not a legacy of Western history, nor is it a "Christian heresy" (the pernicious fallacy popularized by Prof. Toynbee). Essentially, it came out of the East, as a conscious apostasy from the West. It may indeed be said that Jacobinism was its forerunner; but Jacobinism was itself an apostasy from the liberal tradition of the West, as well as from Christianity, by its cardinal tenet (roundly condemned by Pope Leo XIII) that there are no bounds to the juridical omnipotence of government, since the power of the state is not under the law, much less under God. In any case, communism has assumed the task at which Jacobinism failed— that of putting an end to the history of the West. Communism has undertaken to inaugurate a new history, the so-called Third Epoch, that will abolish and supplant what we called the two Western epochs, feudalism and capitalism.

My proposition is that each of these four unique aspects of the Soviet Empire has consequences for American policy. No structure of policy will be intelligent or successful that does not reckon with all of them. Indeed, all our past mistakes of policy have resulted from the American disposition to ignore, or to misunderstand, one or the other of these four unique aspects of Russia.

It would be a lengthy task, although not a difficult one, to demonstrate this proposition with a fair measure of certitude. However, I shall make only two major points.

First, if the Soviet Union be regarded simply in the first of its unique aspects, as a state or power, under precision from its other aspects, there need be no serious conflict between it and the United States. By itself, the fact that a single government rules the Euro-Asiatic plain and possesses the technical competence to exploit its natural and human resources poses no serious threat to American interests. There is no reason why the Soviet Union, regarded simply as a state or power-complex, could not live in decently cooperative harmony with the other world-power, the United States. The American locus of power lies in another hemisphere. Our geopolitical position is secure; so too is theirs. Conflicts of interests and clashes of power would arise, but they could be composed peacefully.

This point needs making in order to disallow the conception that the American-Soviet confrontation is purely a power-struggle between two colossi of power, whose sheer power is reciprocally a threat, one to the other. To see the problem thus, and to base American policy on anxious conjectures as to which power is "ahead" or "behind" in the accumulation of power, is to mistake the problem completely.

The many-sided conflict known, not inappropriately, as the cold war is unintelligible (and therefore must seem unreal) except in the light of the second unique aspect of the Soviet state. It is an *imperium*, a mode of rule, guided in its internal and external policy by a comprehensive systematic doctrine that contradicts at every important point the tradition of the West. Soviet theory and practice stand in organic independence. Only Soviet doctrine makes Soviet power a threat to the United States. Only Soviet doctrine explains the peculiar nature of Soviet imperialism and shows it to be unappeasable in its dynamism. Only Soviet doctrine illumines the intentions of the new messianism that has come out of the East, fitted with an armature of power, and organized implacably against the West.

Here, of course, in the concept of an empire controlled by a dogma, is the sticking-point for the pragmatic American mind. Two questions arise. First, is this concept of the Soviet Empire true? Second, if it is, can the pragmatic mind take in its truth and be guided accordingly in the fashioning of policy? For my part, the answer to the first question is unhesitatingly yes. I am less sure about the answer to the second question. The American mind is consciously pragmatist. When questions can no longer be postponed, they are approached with an empirical, experimentalist attitude that focuses on contingencies of fact. The search is for compromise, for the "deal" that will be acceptable to both parties in the dispute. The notion of action being controlled by theory is alien to this mentality. The further notion of a great state submitting its purposes and action to the control of a dogmatic philosophy seems absurd. The pragmatist mind instinctively refuses to take in this notion or to study its implications.

When, therefore, this pragmatist mind reads Stalin's statement about Soviet doctrine that "there can be no doubt that as long as we are faithful to this doctrine, as long as we possess this compass, we shall be successful in our work," it can only conclude that Stalin must have been somehow "insincere." There is the further consideration that Soviet doctrine is couched in a technical jargon that is not only alien but very boring. The practical man puts it all aside. His distrust of ideas has itself become an idea. What he wants is "the facts." And he rapidly overlooks the essential fact that the purposes and actions of the Soviet Empire are unintelligible without reference to the ideas on which its leaders act.

In his recent book, *The Illusion of an Epoch*: *Marxism-Leninism as a Philosophical Creed*, Prof. H. B. Acton makes this concluding statement: "Marxism is a philosophical farrago." Other scholars, within the Academy and within the Church, after even more extensive studies have likewise stigmatized the Soviet dogma as scientific, historical, philosophical, and theological nonsense. But what matters for the statesman is not that the dogma is nonsense but that the Soviet leaders act on the dogma, nonsense though it be. The evidence for this fact may not be unambiguously demonstrative; no historical evidence ever is. But it amply suffices for a firm case that may be made the premise of sound policy. This is not the place to present all of the evidence. The record runs back to Lenin's signing of the Peace of Brest-Litovsk. But the segment of history immediately succeeding World War II deserves a brief mention.

In 1945, despite her war losses, Russia was on the crest of the wave. She had territorial defense in sufficient depth on all fronts. Fellow-traveling governments controlled the new states, including the crucial salient, Czechoslovakia. In the United States, Britain, and France a mood of general, if not unbroken, goodwill towards Russia prevailed to a degree that was almost pathological. Germany, the old enemy of Czarist regimes, was in ruins, impotent, under a military government imposed by the Allies. The Western nations were disarming at breakneck speed. If Russia's own security were the goal, it had been achieved. If the goal were the fulfillment of an old-fashioned Czarist imperial design, looking to the consolidation of power, it too was substantially complete. Or, if the goal was simply the extension of the new imperialism through international enlistments under the device of the "higher patriotism," looking to what Crankshaw calls the "inconsequent mischief-making of the Comintern," the way to it lay open, and eager wishful thinkers in all lands were busily engaged in enlarging the possibilities of mischief, under hardly any opposition or even serious suspicion.

In any case, one would have expected subtle tactics of restraint. Instead the "tough line" suddenly appeared— ruthless pressure for direct control of the satellites, intervention in Greece (and Persia), obstructive opposition to the Marshall Plan and the Austrian Treaty, the Berlin blockade, and the creation of the Cominform. In consequence, within three years the Kremlin had dissipated its major asset of international goodwill. It created for itself a peril that had not previously existed. A divided and disarmed West had begun to unite and arm itself against the menace now visible, though not yet understood.

Why did all this happen? The only satisfactory answer is that the Kremlin was guided by Communist doctrine. The capitalist powers were well disposed? They could not be; the doctrine holds that the capitalist "camp" is irreconcilably hostile. Constitutional socialist governments would protect the socialist homeland against capitalist aggression? No; the doctrine holds that Social Democracy is inherently untrustworthy and ought to be destroyed, because it only deceives the worker and confuses the issue by its pretension to be a Third Force. World peace is the common goal, through negotiations within the framework of the United Nations? Nonsense; the doctrine holds that the conflict between the two homeland "camps" and the two colonial "fronts" is unappeasable. It is the necessary means to the World Revolution. It will be resolved only by the World Revolution. And in its resolution the methods of force cannot be dispensed with. Finally, the doctrine held that at the end of the War the capitalist "camp" simply had to be in a state of "weakness"; its "internal contradictions" were actively at work, presaging its downfall. By the doctrine, therefore, it was the moment for the strategy of the Revolution, the strategy of forceful aggression.

All this may sound rather silly to the pragmatist. In a sense it all was rather silly. The point is that it all happened. And it only happened because Soviet doctrine decreed its happening.

Moreover, it will not do to say that this dictation of policy and events by doctrine will not happen again; that Stalin is dead; that Russia is "different"; that new men are in charge; that they are realists and opportunists, men rather like ourselves who take the pragmatic view. Russia is indeed somewhat different, but only within the limits of the doctrine. The men in charge are new, but only within the limits imposed by their thorough conditioning by the doctrine. The Soviet leadership is not subject to changes of heart. What is more important (and to the pragmatist, unintelligible), it does not even learn by experience. The doctrine is forever at hand to discount Soviet experience of how the capitalist world acts.

The doctrine casts up an image of the capitalist world that does not derive from experience and is not to be altered by experience. It is a "scientific" image, the product of a science, dialectical materialism, whose basic postulate is that determinism rules the world of human history as well as the world of nature. It is through the distorting one-way glass, as it were, of this deterministic theory of capitalism that the Soviet leaders view what we consider to be the contingencies of the historical world—only they are not seen as contingencies but as determined. So far from altering the scientific image, they are interpreted in such a way as either to confirm

31

it or at least leave it intact. When, for instance, the capitalist world professes its desire to be friendly, just, peaceful, cooperative, etc., such professions cannot but be bogus. Historical determinism will not permit the capitalist world to be other than hostile, unjust, aggressive, and war-mongering. Mr. George F. Kennan has commented, in rather baffled, but still superior, fashion, on "the systematic Soviet distortion of the realities of our world and of the purposes to which we are dedicated" (*Russia, the Atom and the West*, p. 29). Mr. Kennan too views reality through his special glass. Apparently it does not occur to him that Soviet analysts of "fact" really believe in the categories of Marxist-Leninist ideology as instruments of interpretation. Like a good American, he believes that if only the Soviet leaders could be brought to see "the facts," with complete "freedom of mind," all would be well.

It is, of course, not impossible that some basic change may take place in Soviet doctrine. But if it did its repercussions would be felt all through the edifice of power erected on the doctrine; and if they were not checked, the edifice could not long survive. The basic Soviet structure is an indivisible and interlocking whole. It cannot permit itself to be tampered with at any point, save on peril of destruction. Still less can it contemplate changes in the dogmas that sustain the edifice of imperialistic power.

The official atheism is necessary in order that the individual may claim no moral rights against the state and no freedom except within the "collective" freedom of the state. This exploitation of the individual in the service of the state is necessary as the premise of forcing further the gigantic technological development. The cult of Soviet patriotism is necessary to preserve the solidarity of the colonial empire over the more than thirty-five national minorities within the Soviet Union, and over the ring of satellite states, as well as to retain that indispensable adjunct of Soviet imperialism, the motley Fifth Column. The maintenance of the police state makes it necessary there should be "danger from without," from irreconcilable, hostile, aggressive capitalist imperialism. This danger is also necessary to explain to the puzzled inquirer why the state is not withering away. The rejection of the possibility of entirely peaceful evolution to world socialism and the belief in force as the indispensable agent of the Revolution are necessary to sustain the burden of militarization and armament. And the whole edifice rests squarely in the basic Marxist dogma—the conflict of two opposed worlds leading dialectically and deterministically to the World Revolution. Finally, the personal security of the Soviet rulers and the continuing privileges of the "new class" are dependent on the maintenance both of the empire and of the revolutionary doctrine that sustains it. Thus self-interest buttresses belief in the doctrine.

The conclusion is that the Soviet Empire not only has been, and is, an empire controlled by doctrine, but must continue to be such, on peril of ceasing to be itself. Even to speculate about making a basic change in the established doctrine of the World Revolution would be to raise the spectre of the disintegration of the empire. This spectre, we may be sure, will be forbidden to rise.

This fourfold view of the unique reality of the Soviet Empire is the only solid first premise of American foreign policy in foreign affairs and military defense. It is a more intelligent premise than the concept of "world domination" in any of the current understandings or misunderstandings of that phrase. It is also a more comprehensive premise than any analysis of the relatively superficial "facts of power."

The major value of a full view of the unique character of the Soviet Union is that it creates a limited but useful set of expectations on which to base American policy. We need not be left to the resources of improvisation or even to the instinctive reactions of purely practical wisdom—the kind of wisdom that made us enter the Korean War but was never able to explain why we did enter it. The Soviet Empire is governed by the inner laws of its own nature; like any laws they create expectabilities. We may, for instance, expect Communist leadership to yield only to calculations of power and success; force and the prospect of success by its use are the determinants of Soviet action. This expectation would clarify the problem of negotiations. It would suggest that we put an end, as quietly as possible, to the Wilsonian era of diplomacy with its exaggerated trust in world assemblies and in spectacular international conferences. It would further suggest the advisability of direct negotiations with Russia. For instance, if and when any agreement on disarmament is reached it will be reached directly between the Kremlin and the White House, without the confusing assistance of twenty-five additional nations.

Again, a true view of the Soviet Union, as a unique imperialism, would suggest that we cease to confuse foreign policy with diplomatic negotiations. To paraphrase a famous remark, foreign policy is when you know what you want. It supposes that you know the possibility of getting what you want, before you decide that you want it. Negotiation is simply the means of getting what you want. The Soviet Union understands this. For instance, it is a fixed Soviet foreign policy to gain public international recognition of the successes of the Communist revolution as they are racked up. This policy is pursued through "negotiations" at international conferences. These conferences negotiate nothing. Either they simply register the political and military results to date and thus fulfill Soviet policy (e.g., the 1954 Geneva "settlement" on Korea and Indo-China) or they run out in sheer futility after two million words (e. g., the prior Berlin Conference). It is time we, too, learned not to fix our policy by negotiations but to conduct negotiations in order to fulfill our policies. It is time, too, that we laid aside completely the concept of "sincerity" as a moral category, even though it is so dear to a type of Eastern-seaboard liberal mind that believes in nothing else. To inquire into Soviet "sincerity" or to require "sincerity" of the Soviet Union is a complete waste of time.

The chiefly important expectability or "sincerity" is that the Soviet Union will always act on its own doctrine. As the situation dictates, it will employ the strategy of the Revolution or the tactics of the protection of the homeland of the Revolution and of the Revolution's imperialist advances. In either case, since the doctrine is inherently aggressive, it permits no "disengagement." It continually probes for every vacuum of power and for every soft spot of purpose. This is why "disengagement" as an American policy could not be other than disastrous. It would surely heighten the danger of war, most probably by permitting the creation of situations that we could not possibly accept. Only the very opposite policy is safe—a policy of continuous engagement at every point, on all levels of action, by both tactical and strategic moves. At times this policy of continuous engagement might well be enforced simply by variants of the highly effective argumentative technique of the blank and silent stare. The Russians employed it well in the tent at Panmunjom. Turkey has always used it successfully; and West Berlin has learned its value. We still talk too much.

A policy of continuous engagement with the World Revolution does not mean solely a policy of hostility, contradiction, and opposition. Nor is it to be translated primarily into military terms. The engagement can be cooperative, positive, constructive in a number of ways. Here I shall mention only one, because it is so neglected.

Perhaps the most alarming pages in Wolfgang Leonhard's book, *Child of the Revolution,* are those in which he reports the effect had on him by Western newspapers, broadcasts, etc. The effect was nil. In fact, practically everything he heard or read about the West only delayed his break with Stalinism. On the intellectual or doctrinal level the disengagement between West and East seems to be almost complete. Torrents of words are poured out Eastward, of course. But they do not even engage the attention of the East. "Why do they always go on about freedom?" asked one of Leonhard's companions, as he got up, bored to death, to turn off a Western broadcast. "In the first place there is no freedom in the West, and in the second place people in the West do not even know what freedom is."

The young Communist's disgusted comment makes the necessary point. Do people of the West understand what freedom is? Can they intelligently dispute the Communist thesis, that freedom means insight into historical necessity— an insight that is based on scientific theory? (One recalls General Eisenhower and Marshal Zhukov baffling one another in Berlin over the notion of freedom.) Or is it rather the American disposition to dismiss the whole dispute as "impractical," and irrelevant to politics? Or do we think that this basic issue of theory would be settled by distributing (as has been seriously suggested) an avalanche of Sears-Roebuck catalogues in the Soviet Union?

It may be that the Illusion of our Epoch will not be overcome by argument. Certainly it cannot be overcome by force. Perhaps it will succumb only to the enemy of all illusions—time. The fact remains that Communist doctrine is an affront to the Western tradition of reason; and the manner of empire that it sustains is a further affront to the liberal tradition of politics and law that was born of the Western tradition of reason. The further fact is that the West was so late in feeling the affront and still seems largely impotent to deliver against it an effective doctrinal answer, in a moment when a doctrinal answer is of the highest practical importance, not only to the East that will hear it, but to the West that will utter it—immediately, to itself. It may, of course, be that the West has ceased to understand itself. Prof. Toynbee may, in fact, be right in saying that the West now identifies itself with technology, as its cult and its sole export. If this be true, this failure of understanding, leading to a denial, more or less explicit, of the Western tradition by the West itself, would be the fateful "internal contradiction" that might lead to downfall. Ironically, Marx never saw this form of "internal contradiction," though it is the greatest weakness in the "camp" that he opposed.

This may be the place to comment on the basic fiasco of our engagement with communism on the domestic scene. The subject is a bit complicated. It is, of course, not necessary to invoke Communist influence to explain the various stupidities of American wartime and postwar policies. Stupidity itself is sufficient explanation. The pattern of it was set by the American President who was "certain," he said in all good faith, "that Stalin is not an imperialist." The anti-Communist movement, centering on the issue of internal subversion, probably compounded the confusion by transforming issues of stupidity into issues of "disloyalty." The muzzy sentimentalism of the 1945 climate has indeed been altered. Reckon this, if you like, to the credit of those who raised the cry of subversion. Public opinion, in the sense of public passion (which it very largely is), has been transformed. Everybody now mortally hates and fears what is known, rather vaguely, as "the Communist menace." It was "brought home" to them amid great tumult and shouting (only in this way, it seems, can things be brought home to the American people). This was a good thing. At that, by a strange irony, those who were the loudest in bringing the menace home were or are the last ones on American earth whom one would want to see in charge of combating the menace abroad, in the field of foreign policy, where the massive menace lies. By a contrasting irony, many of those who took the sound view in matters of foreign policy were fuzzy on the issue of internal subversion.

In any case, whatever its effect on public emotion, the anti-Communist movement has been fairly spectacular in its failure to contribute to public understanding. The problem of understanding centers on three large issues: What *is* this "thing from the East," what *is* the Western "thing" in the name of which we oppose it, and what were the corrosive forces that were able to create a yawning spiritual and intellectual vacuum within the West, but were not able to fill it, with the result that the "thing from the East" found some lodgment there? Thousands of questions and answers before Congressional committees and bushels of propaganda sheets from patriotic societies have contributed almost nothing to an answer to these questions. In their turn, the forces that opposed the anti-Communist movement have rivaled it in their failure to contribute to public understanding. In considerable part they failed even to speak to the real issues, being content to retire, embattled, behind a rather porous barricade—a concept of democracy as an ensemble of procedures, a legal system of civil rights. It was not strange that in the end the public, with some instinctive feeling that the quarrel wasn't getting anywhere, and had become trivial anyway, should have grown bored with it. Imposed on a prior fiasco of understanding, this was a most lamentable result. The three basic questions still stand.

Even yet the response to Communist imperialism is largely in emotional terms—fear and hatred (or, conversely, pathetic appeals to "understand the Russians") and bursts of brief excitement over every new Communist success, and, for the rest, a last-minute rush to the resources of pragmatism in all its forms (notably including military technology) to meet particular issues as they arise.

This brings up the question that looms so large—the question of armaments and war. The underlying issue is whether a full view of the unique reality of the Soviet empire furnishes any reliable expectations in this critical area. There are several.

Soviet doctrine as a whole dictates a policy of maximum security and minimum risk. Risks can and must be minimum because the dialectic of history decrees that the capitalist world, though still powerful, is decaying and must inevitably disintegrate from within, whereas the forces of socialism are in constant ascendancy and must inevitably triumph. Security must be maximal because at every point the gains made by political or military means must be consolidated as the base for further revolutionary advance. The Soviet Union cannot be provoked into taking risks that exceed the minimum; for it does not act under external provocation but under an internal dynamism. These conclusions, already implicit in the doctrine, are confirmed by all the evidence in the historical record.

We may expect that Soviet doctrine will continue to dictate the same policy of maximal security and minimal risk. This expectation furnishes a measure by which to decide the gravest and most pervasive problem of foreign and military policy, namely, how to balance the elements of security and of risk. We may safely invert the Soviet proportions. Our policy should envisage a minimum of security and a maximum of risk. Only by such a policy can we seize and retain the initiative in world affairs. And it is highly dangerous not to have the initiative. On the premise of this balance we did, in fact, enter the Korean war, which was right. But then we retreated from the premise to a policy of minimal risk, which was a mistake.

Moreover, it would be prudent even to create situations of risk for the Soviet Union—situations in which the risk would be too great for it to take. We may be sure that the Soviet leadership will not risk the debacle of the World Revolution through a major war for the sake of anything less than the soil of the homeland of the Revolution. We may expect that it will yield tactical ground, or refrain from going after tactical ground, if the risk of holding it or going after it becomes serious. But if there is no risk, or only a minimal risk, aggressive policies will be carried through, as they were in Hungary, where nothing was done to create a risk.

At the same time, Soviet doctrine serves to warn us to be wary of the facile persuasion now being spread about that "Russia doesn't want war." There is no reason to believe that communism has been converted to the faith of Social Democracy, which holds that the evolution to world socialism can be wholly peaceful. Any notion that the Soviet Union has tacitly entered some sort of Kellogg Pact is absurd. The use of force, as an instrument of national policy, is still an essential tenet in the Communist creed. By the whole force of Communist "insight into historical necessity" Russia still wants war—the kind of war, in the time and place, that would be necessary or useful to further the multiple ends of the World Revolution, not least perhaps by extending the colonial "liberation front."

Moreover, this same insight convinces the Soviet leadership that the capitalist world wants war. War, like imperialism and aggression in general, is inherent in capitalism. This is a matter of scientific doctrine; the Communist understands it to be so, and he cannot be persuaded otherwise. To admit that the capitalist world does not want war would be to go against the doctrine. It would also be to cancel the "danger from without" that helps to justify the police state and to explain why it cannot yet wither away. In the face of the standing Soviet conviction about the war-mongering capitalist world, it would be doubly absurd to believe that the Soviet Union does not want war.

It is all a matter of the measure of risk that war would entail and of the measure of its usefulness for the World Revolution.

Precisely here, however, the present Communist insight into historical necessity—in the case, the necessity of the use of force to further the Revolution—must be less naive than once it was. It was Lenin's emphatic doctrine that "frightful collisions" must take place between East and West before capitalism is overthrown and socialism installed. Lenin was thinking not only of major wars but of other revolutionary violences. But he did believe in the inevitability of major wars. Stalin too believed that war was inevitable and that it would inevitably advance the fortunes of the Revolution. But this simple faith can no longer stand. One cannot doubt that the Leninist-Stalinist doctrine has been subjected to revision in Communist high councils in the light of the realities of nuclear war. What usefulness would attach to this manner of "frightful collision"? What risks of it should be run?

The results of this revision of doctrine may have been hinted at by Khrushchev at the 20th Party Congress in 1956. He did not refer to the new instrument of frightfulness, the H-bomb. His utterance was cautious. The Communist will not renounce his essential weapon, the threat of force. Nor will he renounce force itself. But he will carefully calculate its uses and its usefulness for his own purposes and on his own premise of policy—maximum security and minimal risk. This manner of calculation is his specialty. Moreover, he will make the conclusions of this calculation serve as the premise of his armament policies. His industry and technology are, after all, largely geared to war—not to war in general but to war as a possibly useful instrument of the World Revolution. To the Communist war is not a game, or a galvanic reaction, or an exercise in righteous anger, or a romantic adventure, or a way to develop the national character, or a sin. It is strictly and coldly a means to an end. And the end is clearly defined.

What conclusions has the Communist come to, what policies has he consequently defined for himself (he always defines his own policies, in what concerns both ends and means), in this historical moment so different from Lenin's—in this our nuclear age? The answer to this question would presumably be an important premise of American policies with regard to war and the weapons of war. The answer should be obvious.

First: All-out nuclear war is not a means of furthering the World Revolution; its only outcome would be the end of the Revolution, in the end of the world; the risk of it therefore must be avoided in the conduct of political affairs.

Second: An all-out surprise attack on the capitalist world, with nuclear weapons, would run a maximum risk of the retaliatory destruction of the Homeland and of the Revolution itself; it is therefore excluded as a strategy of conquest.

Third: On the other hand, the capitalist world is intrinsically imperialistic, aggressive, and bent on military conquest, as its hostile "encirclement" of the Soviet Union shows. It is ready for all-out nuclear war; and, despite its professions, it might launch a surprise attack. Therefore the Soviet Union must be ready for both contingencies. Maximum security requires maximum armament, conventional and nuclear.

Fourth: Military force is still a factor in political affairs, through its use, and especially through the sheer threat of its use. The doctrine of the Revolution—the doctrine of "collisions"—still holds. It will come into play whenever the risks are sufficiently minimal, and the chances of success sufficiently solid. These conditions will be more readily verified when the use of force, including nuclear force, is on a small scale for settling (or aggravating) local disturbances. Therefore small-scale nuclear force must be available in quantity, together with conventional arms. But if the risk appears that the tactical action will be enlarged to the dimensions of strategic action, through the employment of strategic nuclear weapons, it must be broken off, lest the Homeland or the Revolution itself be endangered.

In sum: Major nuclear "collisions" with the capitalist world are not inevitable; on the contrary, they must be avoided, since they cannot advance the Communist cause. World socialism can and must be achieved without major war, by peaceful means—political, diplomatic, economic, propagandistic (this, in effect, is what Khrushchev said in 1956). Adventurism is to be rejected, since it violates the policy of minimal risk. On the other hand, the threat of force is still a valid revolutionary weapon; so too is the use of force itself in determined circumstances. Finally, the Homeland is in "danger from without." Therefore the armament program must be pushed through the whole spectrum of nuclear weapons—large weapons as a deterrent for maximum security; small weapons for use with a minimum of risk.

If this diagnosis of Communist thinking is generally correct, it suggests several conclusions with regard to American thought.

First: The danger of an all-out sneak nuclear attack on the United States has been vastly exaggerated. We have maximal security against it in the Soviet policy of minimal risk as long as the massive deterrent is sustained.

Second: The correlative danger of an all-out nuclear war has likewise been vastly exaggerated. It could only happen as the result of enormous stupidity, basically attributable to a complete miscalculation of Soviet intentions, itself based on a misunderstanding of Soviet doctrine. This stupidity is no more inevitable than war itself.

Third: The danger of limited wars has been underestimated. It seems to be the historical American delusion that no war is worth while unless it is unlimited, waged for "ultimate" causes. There is also the special delusion proper to the nuclear age, that any use of nuclear weapons, however low in the kiloton range, must inevitably lead to world catastrophe. Hence the false dilemma: either to begin with catastrophe or to renounce all use of nuclear force.

Fourth: More generally, the whole concept of the cold war, so called, has been overmilitarized and therefore superficialized. This overmilitarization, combined with the exaggerations noted above, has affected national policy adversely in many respects. Moreover, it has tended to obscure or even discredit the validity of the very concept of the cold war. This too is lamentable, because the concept is fully valid, if it is interpreted in the light of the full reality of the Soviet empire in its fourfold uniqueness. Unfortunately, it has become too easy to say that, since the Communist threat is not primarily military (which is true), it is no threat at all and we should make disengagement our policy (which is completely false). Unfortunately too, it has become too easy to say that, since the United States is sufficiently safe from foreign military aggression (which is true), the real threat is internal Communist subversion (which is false).

Finally: All the confusions in American thinking come to a focus in the opinion that the issue of American "survival" is squarely put to the Department of Defense, supported by the Atomic Energy Commission. This opinion is entirely disastrous. We may be quite sure that the Communist mind, with its realistic and strategic habits of thought, has carefully separated the problem of the "survival" of the Communist Revolution from the problem of war. The Communist leadership has no slightest intention of making "survival" the issue to be settled by force of arms. In fact, it is prepared to abandon resort to arms, as soon as the issue of "survival" is raised. Survival is the one thing it is not willing to risk. In contrast, America is not prepared to resort to arms until the issue of "survival" is raised. Survival is the only thing it is willing to risk. Not the least irony in the current situation is the fact that the West has surrendered to the East its own traditional doctrine, that "survival" is not, and should never be allowed to become, the issue at stake in war.

The major problem put to American policy at the moment is the problem that the Soviet Union has already solved in terms of policy, namely, how to be prepared to use force on all necessary or useful occasions, and at the same time to withdraw "survival" from the issues at stake in the use of force. "The children of this world are shrewder than the children of light in their dealings with their own kind" (Luke 16:9). The children of this world understand better the uses, and the uselessnesses, of this world's darkest thing, force. They are shrewd enough to know that the institutions of this world can be advanced by force, but that their survival should not be put to the test of force.

The irony in the Gospel saying seems to be magnificently fulfilled in the American nuclear armament program. It seems to have been conceived to insure "survival" but not to fight a legitimate war for limited and justifiable ends. Perhaps one should not blame the Department of Defense or the Atomic Energy Commission. They could not get their budgets through the Congress unless they "proved" that "survival" is the issue at stake. And the Congress could not levy taxes on the people unless it "proved" that the "survival" of the people is at stake. But this is moral absurdity, not least because it is military absurdity. We have got the problem of "survival" and the problem of war so mixed up that we may finally be incapable of solving either.

Nor will it do to say that we have been forced into this position by the Communist menace. It would be almost impossible to set limits to the danger of communism as a spiritual menace. It has induced not simply a crisis in a history but perhaps the crisis of history. Its dream of the

Third Epoch that will cancel Western and Christian history and the major institutions of that history (notably the rule of law and the spiritual supremacy of the Church) has gone too far toward realization over too wide a sweep of earth to be lightly dismissed as a mere dream. On the other hand, as a sheerly military menace communism is strictly limited. It is limited in the first instance by its own doctrine. This doctrine has always assigned to military force a real role in the advancement of the World Revolution. Nevertheless, the role of force has always been ancillary, subordinate, supportive of political, economic, and ideological initiatives. Force is to be employed only when the historical moment is right and the military or political risk is minimal. Moreover, there is every reason to believe that in the nuclear age, in which all risks are enhanced most horribly, Communist doctrine has set a still more diminished value on the use of force. By a sort of perverse genius, proper to the children of darkness, it has at the same time set a higher value on the sheer threat of force.

The Soviet Union as a power-imperialism must be confronted by power, steadily and at every point. But when the question is military engagement it is quite false to say that the issue is "survival." And American persistence in thinking this could easily reduce American power to impotence. The real issue is to know how and why "survival" got to be thought of as the military issue, and then to withdraw it from the limited political and moral issues at stake in our military engagement wtih the Soviet Union. It is impossible to think of any other way in which our nuclear armament program can be reduced to rationality—to some sensible conformity to the canons of moral reason (which look to justice in war), and to a hardly less desirable conformity to the rules of military reason (which look to success in war).

The clue to the distortions in the present structure of American policy is deposited in a remark made by the Military Operations Subcommittee in its nineteenth report, submitted on February 20, 1958. It said: "Under present methods of operation we do not know what we are trying to accomplish through military aid." Military aid programs, it added, "are not clearly related to a strategy of defense . . . Logistical plans have not been revised to keep step with strategic concepts and strategic concepts lag behind war technology." The general sense of this judgment, made directly with regard to military aid programs, holds with greater force of our nuclear armament program and its newer adjuncts, rockets and missiles.

The general uneasiness among the public—here at home and abroad—derives from an instinctive sense that America does not know what it is trying to do. And the uneasiness is sharpened by the general knowledge of what we are in fact doing, and have in fact been doing since the Manhattan Project. We are engaged in the exploitation of technological possibilities simply because they are possibilities, in the absence of any clearly defined strategic purposes that would be consonant with the institution of war as a valid instrument for altering the political will of an enemy—in the case, the Communist enemy, whose political will, and whose doctrine on the limited use of force in support of his will, are by no means mysterious or unknowable. The general public senses that this situation is irrational and therefore immoral. And it focuses its deeper fear and its more diffused disapproval on the relatively minor question of nuclear tests.

It is doubtless true that military concepts have always lagged behind weapons technology. The lag was tolerable when the technology was limited. This is not so today. The resources of military technology are unlimited, and there is no principle in technology itself to call a halt to their exploitation. Weapons technology has already gone so far that it has raised the issue of "survival" and thrust it into the problem of war, in defiance of every military rule and moral principle, and in defiance too of every sound calculation with regard to the enemy's will to power as supported by a will to war. It is bad enough when policy and armaments run in opposite directions; as Theodore Roosevelt said, we cannot be a nation "opulent, aggressive, and unarmed." But it is worse when policy runs after armaments, and armaments run after technology, with the pressures of budgetary considerations buttressing the primacy of the technology of multi-megaton weapons, because they are cheaper. An armaments race that may end in war is bad enough, since there is always an element of irrationality in war, even when it is a just war. But an armaments race that seems already to have ended in absurdity is vastly worse, because what is militarily absurd is irredeemably immoral.

It may well be that the pragmatist American mind will not hearken to discourse on the morality of war, especially since it bears beneath its pragmatism the American-Protestant taint of pacifism. However, it might listen to discourse on success in war—concretely, on the kind of success that is politically valuable in the kind of war that is possible or likely, in present circumstances, against a particular enemy, who has a fully constructed "compass" (as Stalin called it) whereby to set his intentions and to direct his action in history, and who, finally, has an articulated doctrine with regard to the limited uses of military force in support of his political will. The moralist, of course, will not object to such discourse on success in war. It forms, in fact, the opening paragraphs of his own moral discourse.

A Discussion

MILLIS: The probabilities are that if we maintain a large strategic Air Force there will be no great war of mass destruction. There will probably not be any important small-scale war. The experience the British and French underwent in Suez is probably the pattern of the future. It would be very difficult today to repeat a Korea. The probability is that war has been eliminated from the relations of states. The thought has been in my mind that America has been operating under a false assumption. Since 1945 the whole of our policy has been conducted on the assumption that we are fighting a war with the Soviet Union. I don't believe this fits the facts of this period. Rather than fighting a war, I believe we are working out a relationship of some other character than can be expressed in strictly military terms. The concept of a cold war with Russia is not a meaningful concept, nor is it a valid concept in dealing with the problems which now actually confront us.

GOLDMAN: We are engaged in building a set of relationships with respect to a world-wide revolution, which is social and economic in character and of which Russia is just a kind of state spearhead. The answer to the question of whether the concept of the cold war is meaningful is therefore no, and our policy has been seriously limited because we have been answering yes.

NIEBUHR: There is a cold war insofar as we have a military contest. We have the proof of its existence in the nuclear stalemate, etc. But this has obscured the second dimension of the problem, which one might call competitive co-existence. The two systems are competitive throughout the world and we have not given this fact sufficient emphasis. Our concept of the cold war makes us emphasize military alliances—which does nothing but alienate other countries—and it is this cold war psychology which has interfered with our political strategy of competitive co-existence. There is a military threat, so you can't say that we can do less militarily; but we should not be so obsessed with it as to ignore the other.

MILLIS: It seems obvious to me that we have applied to our situation vis-a-vis Russia a whole series of concepts that are meaningless, in that they do not fit any external reality. Our problem in the largest possible terms is to establish a viable relationship with Russia—that is, between the two great power centers. We approach the problem with concepts that are contrary to fact, the simplest illustration of this being our conviction that as a free society we could necessarily attain a higher degree of technological development than the Communist dictatorial society. This concept has certainly underlain the policies of the past twelve years and we now know, in the face of Sputnik, that it is completely erroneous.

NIEBUHR: There are frightening similarities between what Khrushchev says and what Robespierre said. The Russians may be modern in a technological sense but they are still ruled by dogmas that are not true to the facts. So far as the concept of the cold war is concerned, there is a companion problem—the concept that Dulles takes continually, that communism is an ephemeral condition that will pass away. This is a dangerous illusion, and it is only obliquely related to the cold war and to competitive co-existence.

BUCHANAN: There are two or three questions here. I take it we agree that the cold war concept has made history—the Marshall Plan, the recent conviction that we must have more education in this country, and so on. Actually the concept goes back to the first World War. There has been a kind of cold war ever since, and it has affected foreign policy. This is one question. The other is whether it originally was a valid concept; that is, that communism was threatening regimes all over the world and still is. If you argue both questions at once, you get into terrible confusion.

BURDICK: I think we would have to answer the question of whether the cold war is a meaningful concept with a yes, in the sense that if the two powers believe they are in a cold war the belief begins to make a substantial part of history. Then we might answer, it is meaningful but not sufficient.

NIEBUHR: Couldn't you say it was insufficient and that all the attitudes it engenders tend to isolate the military factors unduly from the over-all factors of competitive co-existence?

BURDICK: This is the chief deficiency of the cold war concept. One of the groups that has recognized this most quickly is the military itself. They want the concept broadened to involve education, aesthetic choice, religious choice, etc.

NIEBUHR: The original conception of containment, as George Kennan described it, was that if you prevented the expansion of Soviet power by whittling away at it, the despotism would become less onerous and there would be a difference between the original revolutionaries and the second and third generations. Kennan has changed his mind about that. Now, as he explained to the Council on Foreign Relations, the real problem—the political choice we have to face—is whether we are going to sit tight until it might blow up and the Soviets become confronted with a desperate choice which might be dangerous to us, or whether our policy would be of such a kind that there would be inadvertently a loosening not of the Soviet system but of its empire and the Soviets would find themselves by the slow process of history with a disintegrated empire.

BUCHANAN: If you take the interpretation of the cold war in any literal sense, it means in effect that we are at war with Russia. This becomes the premise for almost all of our foreign policy and to a great extent our domestic policy.

NIEBUHR: We are at war with Russia in that sense.

BUCHANAN: This means that we have militarized our society to a certain extent. The recoil effect of the containment policy is that we have become a more military society. We understand ourselves that way. We are at war. Therefore, we do certain things.

NIEBUHR: Containment or no containment, we have militarized ourselves more than we were when we were in security. The containment policy did not do this. The historic situation did it. You can't change the fact that America and Russia have become the great power centers beyond the calculation of any historian.

*   *   *   *   *

CHAIRMAN*: Let us take the next step. Since there are two great power centers, which everybody admits, must their policy inevitably be a policy that can be accurately described as a cold war?

NIEBUHR: Yes and no. All of history proves that in a contest between two powers, whether on the national or the super-national level, unless they come to an agreement the military power is always the *ultima ratio.*

CHAIRMAN: Isn't the clause, "unless they come to an agreement," the real question?

NIEBUHR: They will come to an agreement, let us say, because the balance of forces is perfectly constructed and in addition, today, because they might annihilate each other and thus prefer peace to superiority. But even that peace is determined by the *ultima ratio.* In other words, if we did not have a comparative parity of military power, we would not have the security we have today. This is our dilemma. You can't get out of it by adopting some other policy, because a part of the cold war situation is that we have all kinds of power and prestige in contest with it, including nuclear weapons.

CHAIRMAN: What in your opinion would be the difference between competitive co-existence and cold war?

NIEBUHR: Competitive co-existence is a wider term but it does not exclude the military factor. We cannot exclude it. We simply say that it is there. But we must not take sole cognizance of it because we must take cognizance of all the power and prestige factors involved all over the world.

---

* Robert M. Hutchins

MILLIS: The actual relationship with Russia today is not a relationship of two powers at war, cold or hot. It is the relationship of two powers engaged in competitive co-existence. But we refuse to admit this. If we are going to make a success of a policy of competitive co-existence, we must face it ourselves and realize that it is our policy.

CHAIRMAN: It changes the base of your operations. Your object then is to try to make your own existence a model for the world and not so much to hold in check the developments in another country or to threaten another country. I don't feel any obligation to change my educational ideas, for example, as a result of the Sputnik, because I've always thought American education ought to be serious education. The notion that the Russians have made a great discovery in finding that intellectual power is a national asset is absurd; every serious educator in the United States has thought that for centuries.

NIEBUHR: That's right but it is too isolationist an interpretation, because we cannot make our national existence the model for all nations.

CHAIRMAN: Granted. Molotov, I think, first used the phrase competitive co-existence about 1945. He called it the peaceful competition of different social and political systems. If you take this seriously, it would mean that we would try to develop for this country and for the world the full potentialities of the American system. The net result of this would be that there would be a better chance of beating Russia if she had to be beaten in a military way. If you drop the phrase cold war and change it to peaceful co-existence, which I prefer to competitive co-existence, you alter the tone and the direction of your policy.

BUCHANAN: Can't the question be put another way: Do we understand ourselves properly by understanding our relations with Russia as a war?

NIEBUHR: What we are saying is that it is too narrow to term it a war. It is certainly competitive.

BURDICK: Is it possible to have competitive and peaceful co-existence? Isn't this what happened between the Protestants and the Catholics?

NIEBUHR: The analogy is good. Millis says we won't have war in the present situation because we would destroy each other. In the religious wars it was found that neither could win and so they established a competitive co-existence. They decided to get along with one another. So did Islam and Christianity.

CHAIRMAN: Aren't we agreed that the term cold war is insufficient? Aren't we agreed that it is misleading? If the term is insufficient and misleading, then we come to the question of how we want to describe the situation as we think it (a) does exist and (b) ought to exist.

NIEBUHR: If I understand Henry Kissinger's thesis in his book, *Nuclear Weapons and Foreign Policy,* the administration has concluded that war has ceased in any respect to be an instrument of policy. His point is that if you take this absolutely as a sort of pacifist dogma and the Soviets recognize this to be our policy, they will push us around all over the world. They will not be afraid of the ultimate war, because we have committed ourselves to the fact that there cannot be *any* war. The question is not adequate instrumentalities but the relationship of foreign policy to a democracy. The greater question is that as the hazards increase and the technical details become more complex, can foreign policy be grasped in terms of the whole democratic structure? George Kennan may not be right, but he seems to say that in this era foreign policy cannot be as democratic as we would like.

GOLDMAN: As I understand Millis' position, he is saying that war has become so mutually annihilating that there is not going to be a big war, and therefore we should take things in that context.

MILLIS: I think we have already passed the point where a big war is probable. I can't say it is not possible. There is always the business of the sergeant at a radarscope with his finger on the button. I could not make a hard and fast prediction that there is no possibility of a war. I am saying that the two arsenals have grown so huge and destructive as apparently to rule out a war, at least in the near future, and have deprived us of the function which military force previously fulfilled in international affairs. Therefore, we are faced with a situation where force is a vacuum. That situation is not to my mind accurately described by the term "war". I don't know whether it is possible to see this international situation in terms other than those of a cold war, but I think it is. The profound paradox is that we are manufacturing nuclear weapons so that they shall not be used. That is the standard official argument. Yet you cannot manufacture weapons that will not be used. You have to manufacture them as if they would be used, and you have to train your people as if they are going to be used.

MURRAY: Have we ever been really publicly clear about all of this?

MILLIS: No, we have not, because of the paradox we have never resolved. The suggestion has frequently been made in the past that the only way we can deal with these megaton weapons is to announce to the world that we will never use them unless they are used against us. That seems a logical thing to say. The answer has always been made that we could not dare to do that because that would announce to the Russians that we would not intend to use them. The Russians, satisfied that they were never going to be used on them, would then go off and do anything they please. As long as you regard our relations with Russia as primarily those of a war, that sort of decision is almost inevitable. If, however, you can find some other frame in which to place our relationship with Russia—I don't know how to do it—it is conceivable that you might have a foundation on which both of us could talk, and a decision about the use of megaton weapons could be made in some self-enforcing form.

GOLDMAN: I can easily see the American public saying that the dumping of these weapons on Russia is a moral thing to do because communism is so immoral. Its destruction justifies the action. Part of the difficulty, it seems to me, is that we have assumed officially and unofficially in this country that the American purpose should be to destroy or diminish communism.

MILLIS: That is almost the problem—communism is immoral, there is a real responsibility on our side to see that it is destroyed. When you take that position you have declared war on communism. Then you cannot conduct relations with Communists in any other except a war context. I am asking if that context is the only one we can apply. If we can apply a non-war context with our relations with the Soviet Union, we will have to drop the idea that we are under a moral obligation to exterminate communism. We really have a choice here between either competitive co-existence or cold war as the foundation of our policy. Through considering and deciding definitely for either one or the other policy, we might be able to control the development of the world better than we are controlling it now. The overwhelming outside fact, as I see it, is that under the policies we have followed we are not controlling events in any way that leads anywhere except a total military disaster or a total disaster through Soviet Russian conquest of the rest of the world against our wishes. If present trends appear to end in an inescapable disaster on one side or the other, then we must at least address ourselves to the possibility that these trends can be reversed or can be altered or modified to lead to something else. The only place in which I can see that we can begin to attempt to modify them is by re-examining our own assumptions about the nature of the problem with which we are dealing.

GOLDMAN: We are really dealing with a deep-seated judgment on the part of the American people. I think there are two parts to the judgment and I think we have been operating under them for a long time before the cold war. First, there is a conspiracy abroad in the world called socialism, Bolshevism, etc. This conspiracy is in and of itself immoral. Secondly, it is inherently expansive and is constantly threatening us. By threatening us, it is threatening all of our moral judgments and values. I think we have constantly done things as a result of these feelings which we would consider immoral if viewed in the light of our other standards. We can reverse these feelings in two ways. We can say communism is immoral, but we are going to act as if it is not, or we can say that communism is not immoral, under many circumstances, and in many parts of the world.

CHAIRMAN: What about something in between, that communism is immoral but you are not going to shoot all the Communists?

GOLDMAN: If you take my second point, if I am right in what the American people have been saying, that communism is not only immoral but is a constant threat, don't you therefore have a right to try to destroy it with weapons which you would call immoral under other circumstances?

MURRAY: That raises what is to me the most basic power issue; that is, the failure of understanding. I think it is fairly demonstrable that in this country we have never understood the uses of force or the meaning of power. We have gravitated between the two extremes of absolute pacifism and the use of force as in Hiroshima. One extreme is just as dangerous a guide to policy as the other. If we had a thoroughly conceived doctrine with regard to the uses of force, we would never have built the hydrogen bomb in the first instance because it is not a weapon of war, unless you are going to give to the word "war" a content that is inherently absurd. War has been historically a means of improving a power position. That is all. That is all it can ever be.

MILLIS: You can still build it as a weapon of defense.

MURRAY: Not in the absence of any offensive weapon that would call for such a defense.

MILLIS: What instigated the decision to go ahead with the crash program in the hydrogen bomb was the discovery that we no longer had a monopoly of the weapon.

*   *   *   *   *

CHAIRMAN: War is now defined as a kind of death of civilization. War in the past has never meant that. Therefore, it seems that we have generally decided that we would prefer to live. It seems we have generally decided that if this means we have to let the Russians live, we are willing to let them live, too. Since we want to live ourselves, and hence to let the Russians live, we have got to start to talk about the ways in which we live together and whether it is possible to live together. This would seem to require us to drop as an official objective the annihilation of communism or the destruction of governments that profess to be communistic. You have to let them live or else you will get exploded yourself.

MURRAY: We have been permitting them to live, and they us. It is not a question of whether they live or not. It is the measure of power that they are going to be allowed to have or not to have and how they can be blocked from having it or not having it. It is a problem of power, not life. It can be extended into an issue of life or death of the civilization, if you will, but the problem is not the continued existence of civilization, it is the problem of power.

CHAIRMAN: I was extrapolating the present situation to one of life or death. I view the present situation as that.

MILLIS: How would you state the problem of power?

MURRAY: I would have to start, I suppose, with my understanding of communism and its history and dynamisms as they have become evident. I would have to have some understanding of their power program as well as some understanding of the ideology out of which it was projected. Then I would have to decide just how far the success of this program was compatible with a power program of my own. I suppose we as a nation have to have a power program. I would have to see how likely it is for this power struggle to erupt into violence and where and in what measure. Then, having done that as best I could, I still would not have anything more than a basis of, say, high probability from which to launch national policies of various kinds, one of them being development of military power, another being development of other types of power, and so on. Policy is designed—not entirely but to some extent—in terms of the policy it is trying to counteract.

MILLIS: Your description of the analysis of the power problem is a description of what is going on every day. You can read almost anywhere very carefully detailed analyses on points at which the American foreign policy rubs against the Soviet power policy. This is still no solution to the problem before us. Exactly this type of analysis applied to our affairs has brought us to a dead end or a blank wall in which no course we can now advocate appears to offer us the safety, survival, and security of a free society.

BUCHANAN: It is very important to get at the rationale of this whole thing. There is an inference to be made about the use of force. Force can be used under law, and *is* used that way. It seems to me that we should be talking about making a major treaty with Russia. This is the nearest thing you come to law in international relationships. It has been said here that we are not interested in destroying communism and we are not going to distrust the Russians as a national policy. If that is true, we can make a treaty and the treaty would be the way to hold the rationale that is left.

NIEBUHR: A treaty with Russia is both impossible and unnecessary. Politically it is impossible from our side, strategically it is impossible from their side. What we need is a tacit understanding or agreement rather than a treaty.

MURRAY: There is a problem which has preoccupied this country for thirty years in different forms and focused on different things, namely, can our American republican form of government cope with the situation as it exists. It was raised first of all with reference to the economy. We got over that one. Then it was raised with reference to the conduct of war in the face of dictatorship. We got over that one. Now it is back with us again, quite rightly. I think this is a basic problem.

MILLIS: I started from the rather simple proposition that we are not coping with the situation that now confronts us. As far as anybody can project the tendencies now at work, they cross at a point spelling catastrophic disaster. If that is a fair analysis of the present tendencies, it means that our government for whatever reasons, or our people for whatever reasons, are not coping with them. How should they begin to cope, or how can a group such as this make it more easy for them to cope?

GOLDMAN: What have American leaders been saying about the nature of this danger for the last forty years? It seems to me that they have been saying two things: One is that the danger that is Bolshevism is an immoral danger, and, to quote Mr. Truman, America has no meaning unless it opposes it now and forever. The other thing they have been saying is that this danger is inherently and permanently predatory and expansionist, and if you do not check it, undermine it, and attempt to destroy it, it will destroy you. We here cannot say anything significant about the problem unless we also say something about these two propositions.

NIEBUHR: Felix Morley said in one of his books that empire and democracy are incompatible, and we must do away with empire to preserve democracy. In order to preserve our virtue, we must renounce our responsibilities. That is a very ultimate question, which Christian civilization has always faced and which sectarian Christianity and orthodox liberalism have answered wrongly. That is to say, since responsibility involves guilt and danger, we will be pure rather than be responsible. On the other hand, it is argued rightly that if we use these instruments we will annihilate ourselves not only physically but morally. If the bomb were ever used, I would hope it would kill me, because the moral situation would be something that I could not contemplate. At the same time you cannot disavow its use absolutely prematurely without bowing yourself out of responsibility for the whole generation. That is the character of our moral dilemma.

GOLDMAN: If my understanding is correct of what American policy and American public opinion have been, this would be the answer: The destruction or undermining of Bolshevism is so important that no matter what it cost, you must do it. There is a higher morality. The moral meaning of America is to prevent the spread and power of communism. Therefore the moral question of using these weapons is subordinate to the larger morality. This, I think, would be the public answer.

NIEBUHR: Suppose you eliminate the idea that we were called by God to eliminate Bolshevism from the world. Suppose you assume that we did not have an ephemeral configuration here but something we have to live with for who knows how long. You will still have two problems. You still have the problem of whether we could carry imperial responsibility without losing our democracy and the problem of the moral substance of our civilization with regard to the use of atomic warheads in limited wars.

GOLDMAN: I think we can agree among ourselves that the statement that Bolshevism is ephemeral is false. A third point, it seems, we will have to discuss, namely, that Bolshevism is inherently predatory and expansionist. If this is true, the relentless, remorseless pressure to undermine it, to get it, or otherwise it will get you, must be maintained.

NIEBUHR: Any dynamic historical movement is to some degree expansionist. We were expansionist when we found this continent and brushed everything out of our way.

GOLDMAN: I think what is meant by the word "expansionist" is that communism represents a permanent conspiracy which has as its major objective, by any means whatsoever, the undermining of the governments of the rest of the world. This in definition raises serious questions about what it would mean to make a treaty with them, to negotiate with them, and so forth.

MURRAY: Would it be implicit in what you said that we have got to the point now where we have exaggerated the threat or we ought to re-examine it to see whether we have not exaggerated the threat?

GOLDMAN: My own feeling would be that we have exaggerated. We must face the question whether this popular point of view toward communism is the correct one.

* * * * *

CHAIRMAN: Suppose we assume that the Russian threat is precisely what the worst threateners or threat-fearers think it is. Have the methods we have been employing to meet this threat been rational? That is, have they been effective, and have they been in their application in this country and elsewhere just?

MILLIS: There has never been a careful examination and re-examination of the nature of the threat. We have never stopped to say, what is the threat? Is it the threat of a sudden sneak attack with atomic weapons to be delivered on this country at any moment without any warning? I think it is quite possible to say that is a remote element of the threat. It is almost unimaginable that it will ever actually happen. A State Department official has made the flat statement that the Department had decided that the policy of the Soviet Union was not to start a war but to avoid a war. Meanwhile, however, building up of armaments would permit them to continue their other policies without inciting war. Their whole effort was to prevent these other policies from resulting in a war, either a big war or a little war. That is a very logical analysis, it seems to me, of the fundamental nature of the Soviet policy. Now, if that is the nature of the threat, it makes it all the more plain that many of the things we have been doing have not in fact been rational means to meet the Soviet threat.

NIEBUHR: The question would be whether it is a threat of world domination or whether it is calculated expansion wherever there is a weakness militarily or economically for them to fill the vacuum. That is the nature of the threat.

BUCHANAN: Any live element of history is expansionist. If it falls into a certain pattern, it is conspiratorial. That is where we are. It seems to me we ought to be able to get above that. Accept the conspiratorial thing as we accept the cold war. This is relatively true at present. We made it true. By acting against a conspiracy, we have become a conspiracy and this has become a vicious pattern. Can't we get above that somehow? Isn't the reciprocal position here something very familiar in history; that is, any two powers in history have always been enemies in some sense, they have been expansionist, they have been subversive to each other? There is nothing new about this.

CHAIRMAN: Where do you come out?

BUCHANAN: With a treaty. If you drop these assumptions which are obviously only half-true and perhaps terribly false because they are half-true, you get to that. Niebuhr says it is politically impossible. It is politically impossible because no group like this has ever said to the contrary.

NIEBUHR: The analogy between Hitler and the Russians is the most false analogy we have to deal with because Hitler had to have military expansion in order to exist at all. The Soviets are expansionists in a quite different sense. They are politically, morally, and ideologically expansionist. You cannot get rid of this by simply destroying them. Here is where Kennan's point comes in. The ultimate choice is whether we want to drive them into a corner where they will become desperate or whether we will create a situation where the empire will disintegrate, and disintegrate so inadvertently that the Communist oligarchs themselves can't deal with it.

GOLDMAN: My understanding is that the consensus of this group is this: There is a popular view that communism is inherently expansionist to the point where you cannot deal with it. You cannot do business with it. We agree that this view is not necessarily correct.

*   *   *   *   *

MURRAY: It seems to me we are piling assumptions on assumptions. We are assuming that it is the assumption of American foreign policy that a political objective of the United States is the utter destruction of the Soviet empire. Is our assumption that this is the assumption correct? I am inclined to say it is not.

GOLDMAN: I would state that this has been a major assumption.

MURRAY: Maybe you have to distinguish. There are two things constantly going on in American life which necessarily must go on because of the nature of the threat. We cannot view with complacency a reign of tyranny all over the earth. What we do about it is something else again. My judgment on the damnation that I invoke on the tyranny is one thing. The action I propose to take against the tyranny is quite something else again. It is on this second level that I would conceive foreign policy to rest. You have the two levels very clearly demonstrated—and also the impasse which the failure to join them leads to—in the Hungarian situation. The air was filled with moral denunciations. Apparently nobody ever thought antecedently what we possibly could do as, if, and when such a situation arose. We had no policy.

GOLDMAN: I wonder whether a detailed history of U.S. policy from 1947 on would bear out the sharp distinction you make between the power level and the prophetic level. It seems that the two things were constantly confused in the minds of those who were making policy. I should say that if we had not been operating upon the prophetic assumption as well as the power assumption our foreign policy would have been very different.

MURRAY: You are probably right. The confusion of these two things has been at the root of a lot of our confusion in foreign policy. The notion of confusion, the level of moral judgment, the level of policy formation are all related to the basic failure of both moral and political intelligence in the national relationship, which is force.

BUCHANAN: You are separating these too sharply. Do you mean to be going as far as you are?

MURRAY: Separating what?

BUCHANAN: The moral and the power judgments.

MURRAY: I don't want to separate them. I say we in our day-to-day national fumbling-around have separated them. I don't want them separated.

BURDICK: I would like to see them separated. I think this is what Goldman suggested. He made two statements; one is a moral statement, the other is a statement about reality. The moral statement is that communism is evil. The reality statement is that it is expansionist and impracticably so. I think these two should be kept separate.

MURRAY: One of the moral factors to be considered in the use of force is the pragmatic factor of success. There must be a reasonable chance of success in the power arena, otherwise the action is not fully moral.

BURDICK: The distinction between morality and morals can be reduced to more manageable questions: Is extinction of communism as an ideology desirable? I think the answer in America would be yes. Is the extinction of Communists as persons desirable? Here you would get some ambiguity. Under some circumstances, for example, as a defensive move we might be prepared to drop bombs to exterminate Communists as persons. The third question would be, is the extermination possible? Clearly here, the answer is yes. Fourth is the extermination possible without ourselves being exterminated? Apparently the answer is no. The fifth question would be, does the fourth question affect the morality or the expediency of the previous questions? After we had answered these, then we might be able to find practical working alternatives. These questions deal with both the morality and the reality of the situation, and keep them distinct.

* * * * *

CHAIRMAN: It has been suggested that we might be at the point where a treaty with Russia covering all outstanding issues might be seriously considered. I would like to ask Mr. Berle his view of the relative value of one procedure or another.

BERLE: I do not see how any treaty or agreement with Russia could be effective if you assume that Russia is going to continue her general desire to conquer the world. I am afraid that any American-Russian agreement now, in the present state of affairs, would be certainly broken and the next step is war, as happened after the Munich Pact and the Hitler-Stalin Pact. There is only one question that is basically unsettled. That is whether the Soviet Union is going to try to use its combined political and military techniques to establish something narrowly approaching the word "empire." They accuse us of the same thing. I think we would agree that is not true of us. I think it *is* true of the Soviet Union. We are not going to settle that by sitting down together and talking it over.

NIEBUHR: We are in a very great dilemma. We cannot overcome it simply by saying that if we abandon the false psychology of a cold war we can negotiate on all things and get into a scheme of competitive co-existence. Khrushchev has spelled it out the way Eisenhower spells it out. He has said, of course, we don't want war, but the imperialists do want war and we have to have a deterrent power against imperialists. This is exactly what Eisenhower also says. We both have the same policy. That is the pathos of the dilemma.

BERLE: I can't see the cold war as a fantasy. The bullets that were coming across the fields in 1948 and 1950 and 1956 looked to me like perfectly real bullets. In the first place, instead of saying there is not a war, I would like to say quite frankly there is one. It may be the word is inept. Second, I would like to say we may have reached the point at which there is a possibility of an armistice or of a policy looking towards an armistice. We have certain limitations. We cannot bargain with the rights of other people. When Kennan and Millis say let Middle Europe go, I find myself interested in liberation as a moral dilemma which I am totally unable to solve; that is, our inability to bargain with the lives of many tens of millions of people. However, let us leave that alone. There may be a possibility of working towards an armistice.

Third, there are a group of fundamental considerations on which I think we and the Soviet Union agree. What are they? One is that there is a common desire in both populations not to have this thing go to ultimates. That I think is as true in the Soviet Union as it is here. Another is that the economic burden of the modern armament race is going eventually to break either system if carried to ultimates. We match the Soviets and can match them, and in any such matching operations their system becomes increasingly impossible and possibly ours, too. So there is a common motive to bring this situation under some control. Fourth, I think we have inadequately communicated the degree of common ground we have with the Russians or with the Soviet statesmen. I think we could make it perfectly clear that no American would spend a dollar, let alone a life, to try to change the system in the Soviet Union by force. The idea that they are constantly under attack, which they have sedulously fomented, is a myth, and we ought to be able to communicate that. If we start there, then we have to add a limitation where we do not agree. The first is that we cannot bargain away the rights of any other people. We can concede, if we like, that our own system is not the only system by which other peoples can organize their affairs. In other words, we do not consider this a competition between different forms of industrial organization. Actually, our systems are so alike when you bring them together—I mean mechanically and organizationally—that you discover the competition is not between two social systems, it is between the content of either system. At this point we then get down to cases. An exploration of those cases conceivably might lead to a basis for armistice. I mean just that, a temporary cease-fire.

Finally, I would like to see if we could not throw on the screen the fact that we are not trying to recreate the nineteenth century with the United States playing the part of Britain. It cannot be done any longer. To say you can "accommodate" doesn't take you anywhere. If accommodation means anything, it can only mean some kind of work-out in a few specific situations which you hope would enlarge themselves by the painful process of beginning with limited common ground and finding out where it can be expanded. The philosophy or at least the publicly stated philosophy by which all these matters have been tackled has been absurd. It seems to me any time Khrushchev says something that is decent and human we ought to recognize it. Every step he takes that looks toward a decent recognition of what we call human rights we ought to accept and welcome. We don't need to add that we think he is a liar. He may be, but the essential question is the political effect of what he says or does. In any case, instead of having rebuffed every apparent movement towards our point of view, we should have welcomed it. For example, we could have recognized the one thing that I think ought to have been recognized—that Khrushchev (who is not any great favorite of mine certainly) did move towards liberating a great many of the political prisoners. To say that every decent thing the Soviets do is just propaganda is merely silly.

CHAIRMAN: Our purpose, as I understand it, is to produce a state of mind in which instead of saying, let us get bigger bombs so we will be able to blow up more people even though this means we will get blown up ourselves, we say let us figure out whether we can do something about this Polish loan, for example.

BERLE: Stopping the arms race is contingent on beginning to get gradual understanding on the other side. I am firmly of the opinion that you will never get any cessation in the armament race until you get some cessation of the opinion that each side is merely waiting for the moment to do the other side in. We believe that is wrong when applied to us and right when applied to the Soviet Union. I may add that I think the evidence against the Soviet Union adds up to a pretty powerful bag of evidence, but they have to determine, I think, as we do, whether they want to keep up with this effort.

* * * * *

NIEBUHR: Could I suggest that we would perform most effectively not by confessing absolute guilt on all levels of our policy but simply by analyzing the predicament in which we and the Russians are. How similar it is! What makes our policy so wrong is that we assume we are always right. We can offset our reputation not only with the Russians but with our allies of being inflexible, self-righteous, and so forth by calling attention to the fact that we are in a common predicament and we ought to recognize it. We are in a common predicament in regard to the burden of the arms race. We are in a common predicament in regard to preserving our strategic security. We are in a common predicament in relation to the political and economic realities of Asia and Africa today. That is where Dulles is so wrong in regarding communism as an ephemeral thing which will blow up if you keep the heat on. We should say that we are dealing with a viable social system which we think is dangerous to the world but which has certain powers of attraction in Asia and Africa. We are in the same predicament in regard to the fact that Russians believe they are the wave of the future and we believe we are the wave of the future. The technical collectivism of Soviet power is more attractive to Asia and Africa than our curious libertarian ideas which are not as libertarian as we say they are. We have not proved that this liberty is compatible with justice and stability.

MILLIS: The fact is that we have two super-states, neither of which can destroy the other and both of which are related to their surrounding people in various ways. The picture of a war between the angels of light and the angels of darkness, between light and freedom and darkness and enslavement doesn't fit the facts of international history.

NIEBUHR: It does not fit the facts to say that if we get rid of the war psychology, these things would be solved. We are in a war. It is not militarily dynamic in the way that Napoleon or Hitler was. That is a false analogy. But it is dynamic. It is dynamic primarily in a political sense and an economic sense. Khrushchev disassociates himself from all analogies with Hitler and says, "Why should we have war? We have this vast expanse of territory." That is indeed a fact. That is the difference between them and Hitler. They have what they want, in effect, and a war would annihilate everything. Khrushchev says, "We have the future on our side. Why should we bring the world to disaster by military action?" Granted we can't trust him altogether on this. Communism has a broad political base. It has an ideology that regards itself as the wave of the future, but it has not the historical military necessity of getting more territory in the way Hitler had to get territory in order to survive at all. The basic mistake in our policy is to regard Hitler and communism as identical forms of dictatorship. It is basically true that military weapons are ancillary to their purposes and not primary; with Hitler it was the other way around.

BERLE: The present state of American policy is that we have expressed our willingness, and are committed, to explore through diplomatic channels with the Soviet Union any matters which might conceivably be agreed upon at a possible conference, summit or otherwise. If you are perfectly certain that anything they achieve on their side is done primarily or solely for the purpose of abuse, you would enter negotiations in a rather different frame of mind than if you assumed that Poland is a problem to them as well as to us and perhaps there is some possible *modus vivendi.*

*   *   *   *   *

BURDICK: I think there are three substantial errors in Father Murray's analysis. First, he assumes that communism has a character that is fairly stable, rigid, and unchangeable. Second and most important, that we can study this and come to know the essential character and personality of communism. Despite the fact that Dr. Niebuhr and other people tell us there is a great scholarly debate about this and it is almost inscrutable at this time, Father Murray makes it clear that he believes that when we know the character of communism we will discover it to be evil because it is antagonistic and destructive of the character of man; it is imperialistic. The third assumption is that having discovered that the personality is evil we can construct a foreign policy on this basis. I think that none of these three is relevant to our discussion. I agree that the character of communism has little bearing unless we can do something about it. I think it is clear that today, regardless of what the character of communism is, there is very little that we can do about it and that our present way of dealing with it has some consequences that we can calculate pretty accurately.

NIEBUHR: Whether communism is evil or not is ultimately irrelevant if we agree that something must be done. Take the religious wars after the Reformation. There is no question that the Protestants regarded the Catholics as evil and vice versa, because Protestantism represented an anarchy and

Catholicism represented tyranny. The point is that neither could overcome the other and so they finally reached a competitive co-existence and they have lived that way ever since. That is an historical analogy.

LUCE: I take as my text the sentence: "If we believe in ourselves we need only stand upon our own convictions, looking to our freedom, power, and creativeness to determine the course of history." And in that sentence I take the words: "stand upon our own convictions." What do we mean by "convictions"? I would suggest that convictions are compounded of three elements. One is vision, the second is principles, and the third is circumstances. Let us say, vision and principles confronted at any given moment, and always, with circumstances. Circumstances have to be observed and assessed and you agree or disagree with what they are when vision and principles confront them. By vision I mean Isaiah's use of the word: "Where there is no vision, the people perish." By principles, I mean political philosophy in general, in the sense in which we say the principles of the American form of government or something of that sort. I make a distinction between vision and principles. Principles are susceptible to a coherent statement and to agreement or disagreement. Vision, which is quite as important as principles, perhaps more so, is not as susceptible of semantic articulation. A man or a group of men or possibly in some sense a nation has a vision of how the world may be, a vision of what the ultimate meaning of man may be. The case of the United States is almost unique in its expression of political principles. I do not say it expresses them well, but they are susceptible of more exact analysis than a statement of what might be called vision. Now, let us look at the circumstances and see how circumstances alter the cases or how devotion to principles may alter circumstances.

BURDICK: Wouldn't you say that the American society is anti-visionary and pro-principle? One aspect of our constitution is that we do not want to provide ways in which visions can become official or single. You can search for the vision any way you want. This is the first of our principles.

LUCE: I think you are right that what Americans feel they should hold in common and fight about in common is the form of government and how you work this form of government out. Whereas, for example, something like a religious unity is not supposed to be the American task.

NIEBUHR: That is Burdick's point, that we assume a plurality of visions.

GOLDMAN: Mr. Luce, I am much attracted by your idea that we ought to try to figure out and then state what we stand for, but I am worried by what I take to be the implication in your remarks that if we did that we would achieve something good for the United States. What I have in mind is this: I will go out on a limb and venture what seems to me the basic American principle about the world, which is that there is a kind of law of history about the world. This is what I think Americans believe: That all peoples everywhere want peace and democracy and that the reason they don't have it is that evil men have come in and deprived them of it. This, I would say, is a basic American principle drawn in fact from our history. What bothers me is that if you and I could agree that this is a basic American idea the thing that is wrong with it is that it is wrong. History has not worked that way. What is going on in the world today is the proof that it has not worked out that way. This is the American delusion, if you will. Should we not state to the world that we have been operating under a delusion?

LUCE: You are jumping too fast. It is by no means to be presumed that most of the rest of mankind responds to this kind of statement of principle. They may not even be the right principles, ultimately, for the world, but they are our principles.

NIEBUHR: Isn't it important to make the distinction between vision and principles? The principles upon which we are founded are the principles of a pluralistic society that grants freedom and toleration within its pluralism. The vision that we have is this pluralistic society as an example for all the world to follow if they were not evil or ignorant.

GOLDMAN: The word "vision" is a laudatory word. Don't we have to raise the issue whether what we have is a vision or whether it is a kind of egocentric projection of our own ideas on other people?

LUCE: I think it is important to find out what a group of Americans believe about American principles.

CHAIRMAN: Will you extend this to apply to Millis' statement? This would mean, as I understand it, that in this statement you would try to indicate what the principles were for which Americans stand. You would then discuss our foreign policy in the circumstances in which we find ourselves possessing these convictions. Is that correct?

LUCE: That is just what I mean.

MILLIS: May I ask this question: Suppose we did establish an agreed statement of American principles and American vision. Do you conceive that the terms by which that statement was established would have a material effect on the paper I have drafted; that the manner in which you state your principles and vision would affect the pragmatic steps you take?

LUCE: Yes.

NIEBUHR: If you state it purely in moral terms or political terms, something is left out. The idea of circumstances is integral to principles. How do you state principles in the context of circumstances? So you can't state principles clearly except where they are inconclusive and pragmatic. What does a free society mean in the light of the circumstances that we are in competition with the Soviets in areas of Africa and Asia where our kind of free society does not quite make sense and where the Soviets' kind of collectivism is dangerous? There the circumstances tell more than the principles. Isn't it futile to go into the historical analysis of what our vision is? Take Mr. Luce's statement of the two visions we had. One is that we were the idea of democracy and other people could take an example from us. Then, beginning with Woodrow Wilson, we say we must export this. Those are two visions of the relationship of America to the world. They were both illusory. They were the visions that an immature nation had both of its power and of its ideals in the vast context of world history.

LUCE: It was not simply a fantasy. The American experiment by accident or providence has made a kind of breakthrough. Other people do want it and will tend toward it.

BERLE: I agree that if you tried to make a statement of a vision you could not do it. We would like to have several visions going. But we do have a vision of a society, if not a government, which regards the holding of visions as sacred and endeavors to give the widest base of political and economic materials so that they can be realized. That is one thing. The second is that we try to construct a government of our own responsive to people for that precise purpose. That is why we do it. We rather look forward to an international world system which does the same thing. When it comes to what you could give up out of this in the interest of accommodation, the only thing you could discuss is form. That is, free elections might be a good way or a bad way of achieving representative government; but you could not give up the hope that the government or governments with which you were dealing were essentially trying to allow visions to constitute themselves instead of crushing every other vision but their own.

GOLDMAN: Mr. Berle, would you accept the interpretation of what you are saying along these lines, that there is a kind of fallacy of Westernism in this thing? Through democracy one achieves a social and economic uplift of the masses. This is what Western society has assumed and, particularly, our society. We have projected a vision of the world in those terms and it has not worked out that way. Democracy does not seem to be the road to social and economic change. It does not seem to be the wanted road.

BERLE: I am prepared to say that at any given point or period on the map or in time democracy may not work. But I don't believe we need to abandon the hope that in the long period of time it will prove to be the most effective. Pragmatically we think it is pretty effective for us.

GOLDMAN: When we are stating principles to the world, do we not have to decide whether we believe that you can get desirable social and economic change only through democratic methods? One of the great confusions in our policy lies exactly in that area, I would say.

NIEBUHR: I don't see how you could clarify that confusion absolutely. On the one hand, democracy is an absolute necessity of justice and on the other hand democracy is a luxury which is attainable only by a highly technical and very balanced society. These two things do not quite fit. You have to spell them out if you are talking about them.

BERLE: An elected democracy in a state in the middle of Africa may be of blazing irrelevance. I should imagine it would be. This is not to say that you do not still anticipate as a part of your vision that that state in due time will be the kind of society which can handle democracy or something like it.

GOLDMAN: Suppose you get a circumstance abroad where through totalitarian methods the general population is being socially and economically benefited. Do you not have to decide whether you consider the vision of democracy more important than you do the vision of social and economic change?

BERLE: Yes.

GOLDMAN: That is all I am asking.

BERLE: But I think there you are picking a different range of time. The totalitarian society may be able to bring a society from "X" to "Y" very rapidly and then leave it in a mess. Let me add that one synthesis ought to be made and has not been made. The fact is that there is no demonstration yet that a totalitarian society can do it more rapidly.

MILLIS: I don't see how restating our principles in any terms is going to contribute anything to the process which I think most of us agree must somehow be brought about; that is, a relaxation of the military struggle between the Soviet Union and the United States. While we hope that the world will ultimately conform to democratic principles, the most we can see as of now, probably, of attainment is a solution similar to that arrived at between the two great religions in the sixteenth and seventeenth centuries.

LUCE: An attitude which the United States might want to take, which might be good for fifty years, would be that we insist that no power control the earth. Never mind whether there is ambition or not. We will take steps and measures to be sure that no power of any sort, whether it is the aviator kings or the Kremlin, should control the earth. I would like that much better than to say we will settle for half the earth or a quarter of the earth and you have the rest.

BUCHANAN: I am sorry if I misunderstand Mr. Luce, but it seems to me he is talking about ideology and not political principles.

LUCE: Ideology is propaganda.

BUCHANAN: It is propaganda to yourself, too. You are trying to make yourself believe it. This has been going on for twenty years. All of us are aware of this. Sometimes there is a very explicit American appeal to the public: let us have an ideology so we can meet the other ideologies in the world. It seems to me too bad. We should be able to do something else. Our fundamental rules come from the common man. Every human being is born free and equal. That is where we derive our just principles of government.

In foreign relations and in military affairs we have to find some channel by which these fundamental rules can become operative again. At present we are all sickened and confused and feel helpless about the whole situation. Although you may have simple-minded convictions, there is no way they can get processed through the government and the appointed officers and all the rest. We in this group ought to be concerned about this. We ought to be concerned about processing the ordinary man's principles of conviction that arise from his own soul and formulating and communicating them to the public; in other words, setting up a process by which the common convictions of the ordinary man can be put into international relations.

LUCE: The American common man seems to be voting more than he used to. You think that the election process is failing very seriously to work?

BUCHANAN: I think voting is a very important function, but the ordinary processes of persuasion are much more important. That is the only thing that makes voting mean anything. Our persuasion has been cut short. This has to do with civil liberties and things like that that have failed in the last ten years. The military thing has destroyed a lot of our persuasive process. This is true on all levels—public meetings, free association, and everything else. We have destroyed our fundamental persuasive processes and therefore cut off our government from our own convictions and, vice versa, almost allowed them to overwhelm us.

*   *   *   *   *

CHAIRMAN: As I understand it, you are proposing that we make a moral judgment ourselves which may articulate the moral judgment of the people. How would you make the argument?

BUCHANAN: It would be a statement of some things that Mr. Luce refers to when he says our convictions.

CHAIRMAN: Such as?

BUCHANAN: Our general behavior in international relations. The idea that we are out to destroy foreign governments is not part of our deep conviction at all. On the contrary, there is a very deep conviction that we should not do that. Take also the idea that we should think that Russians are liars, in terms of either the diabolic notion or Kennan's notion that they have forgotten how to tell the truth. Although there is a great deal of evidence toward it, this seems to me fatal to all our negotiations with them. There is no chance of getting along with them at all. It is an incitement to them to do more of what we object to. I am afraid we catch the same thing. We begin lying, too. This seems to be going on on a grand scale. The main aim is to get the Russians into the world community. If you consider them outlaws and all the other things we call them, there is not any hope for peace at all. This is absolute barbarism on our part.

NIEBUHR: I would agree with the end, but the worst possible way of reaching it is to trust them, because trust is developed by all kinds of communal processes which have to be established first. You do not establish the process of truce in a community by trusting first. You live together on various levels. The main thing is that we have our principles. We state our principles or ideologies or visions or what have you. It must also be recognized that an atomic war is possible, and that the Russians and we both know this to be a fact. Therefore, we must adjust ourselves to both a nuclear stalemate and an ideological stalemate. This ideological stalemate might not be trust or mistrust. It was not between Catholics and Protestants. It was simply a gradual living together. There grew out of this living together a certain trust that you don't establish by challenging people to trust each other.

BUCHANAN: I have some difficulty in seeing the difference between living together and trusting each other.

CHAIRMAN: Let me ask you, Dr. Buchanan, whether this is equivalent to what you were saying: That we should deal with the Russians and we should not on all occasions proclaim that we don't trust them.

NIEBUHR: That I will accept.

* * * * *

MILLIS: I sense the existence of an issue which seems to be very fundamental in the discussion which has been going on here. One group here feels that the Communist world is a fact and our primary problem is to work out a system of negotiation with this world. In order to do so, we have in a large measure to accept it in the same degree, let us say, that Christianity finally accepted Islam. The other group here says that we can never accept the Soviet Communist world as it is now, that it is fundamentally aggressive, it is fundamentally evil, it is fundamentally contrary to our principles and philosophy of life.

CHAIRMAN: It seems to me that those who take one view of communism and those who take another, and there are shades of these views, agree that the ultimate holocaust has got to be avoided. It can be avoided only by dealing with the Russians, and this has to be done without constant proclamations of our distrust of them. If this is a general agreement it is most important, because it means that a national policy which falls into two parts—(a) every opening that is offered is slammed shut from our side, and (b) we talk almost entirely in terms of bigger and bigger armaments in order to blow up these people—these policies are in the opinion of this group unsound.

LUCE: I would like to suggest the case of Poland today. I am speaking of the Catholics, and the position of Cardinal Wyszynski. There you have a very good case of living together. There is no acceptance on the part of Wyszynski or the Vatican of any Communist ideology. There is an acceptance of Poland by Gomulka and Wyszynski. They are both for Poland.

NIEBUHR: I think that example is splendid. They have one thing in common: Poland. We have one thing in common: the saving of the world. We try to get along with each other because we want to save the world, as they want to save Poland. Take the orthodox and secular Jews in Israel. They don't trust each other at all. They have a common interest in Israel which holds them together. They had so little trust of each other—an archaic orthodoxy and complete secularism—that they could not write a constitution. That is why a covenant between Russia and ourselves is impossible because you have to spell out in what way you will protect yourself against the other guy. The Israelites could not establish a constitution. Why? Because some wise people said this thing has to settle down. If we try to write a constitution now, we will try to protect ourselves against you in such a way that we will just get into a fight with one another. But we have to live together. They have accommodated themselves to each other.

BUCHANAN: I am not talking about a constitution. I am talking about agreements. I am saying we should be willing to enter agreements properly formulated and processed. I am talking about a certain attitude that we have, that it is dangerous to come to any agreement with the Russians.

NIEBUHR: It is more important to have understandings than agreements. What we have to do is to reach understandings on all levels without explicit covenants because we haven't got enough trust.

*   *   *   *   *

LUCE: It is an obligation of the United States, which has been unfulfilled so far, to develop and project certain ideas, proposals, and suggestions as to how the world community should be. If we are able to say what America stands for and what our convictions are and then examine the question of America's relation to the world, it becomes not only our duty but our nature to develop a type of world community in consonance with these principles, making compromises or whatever in accordance with our ethos, in accordance with our understanding of other people. I would say, let us have a little less emphasis on the Russians. I am not forgetting the gun they have in their hand or the size of it. We had better proceed with our guard up, as the saying is, as an aim to make a mutually good agreement here and there, but we should be trying at the same time to develop a reasonable and in some sense a radically new world system. As we develop our own ideas and get agreement or partial agreement with other countries, always implicitly there will be the invitation to the Russians to join that developing world community in such a way as suits them. We should not make our idea of how to settle the world depend on what the Russians say.

BERLE: The crushing thing that we have to meet is really what was called old-fashioned imperialism. That is the real reason why you have distrust, and the fantasy, which is unhappily not a fantasy, of the cold war. It is that we are trying to allay by trying to find some method of getting inside the Soviet complex to convince them of two things: First, we don't intend to change their social organization. That is their business. We do regard as hostile anything that undertakes to be hostile to us. Next, our vision of the world is totally upset when the Soviet Union imposes its vision of the world in the singular ungentle way it has done on others by force. This is really about where we start and stop.

MILLIS: I think a very strong argument can be brought out that an alteration in our present foreign policy will make the total destruction less and less likely and will bring us nearer and nearer to a time when we can escape the overwhelming threat. I see an extraordinary and unique opportunity, one that has never occurred in the past history of international relations. Because the destruction is bound to be so total, because everybody knows it—the Russians as well as ourselves—we have an opportunity for normalizing international relations in a way they have never been normalized in the past.

BERLE: I wonder if there is not agreement on this: The present situation is unsatisfactory, and unless some way is found to change the pattern we don't see it getting any more satisfactory. We are, therefore, looking for some way of shifting the pattern of affairs. The only way we see is to take advantage of the present apparent stand-off, if stand-off there is, to try to see what measures of accord can be found, if any, from which an abatement of the arms race can proceed. Summed up, isn't that about what it comes to?

*   *   *   *   *

BUCHANAN: I would like to ask Father Murray a question. It seems to me that when you accept dialectical materialism and the messianic theory that goes with it, and assuming that it is really effective in Russia, you are caught in a kind of paradox. That is, you are in a sense admitting the truth of the doctrine.

MURRAY: The question of the objective truth of the doctrine is, of course, the central issue.

BUCHANAN: Do they act in accordance with it?

MURRAY: That is my thesis, that they do, substantially.

BUCHANAN: Then you are admitting a peculiar kind of truth. I wonder if you want to accept it.

MURRAY: In the first instance, I am admitting simply a fact; the fact that this particular instrument is in control of both their purposes and their actions.

BUCHANAN: Suppose you run across a man in a hospital who believes he is Napoleon. Do you assume he is Napoleon and will act that way?

MURRAY: If I were his keeper, I think I would assume that he would act in accordance with his own inner view.

BUCHANAN: Suppose you believe that the Soviet doctrine is false. Then they will be behaving in a peculiar way which will not follow from your assumptions if you assume that they will follow their own doctrine.

MURRAY: That I don't see. Whether the doctrine be false or not, it tells them to do this or that. Therefore, when I put myself in their context, I may expect them to do this or that, and what I want to know on the level of statesmanship is what they are going to do, not whether or not their theory is capable of substantiation.

BUCHANAN: It does not seem to me that the Russian doctrine is failing.

MURRAY: Whether or not they are following the doctrine, there is the further argument whether or not the doctrine is true.

BUCHANAN: I think they are connected. They can't follow it if it is not true.

MURRAY: They can't follow it? All I say is that I think they have.

BUCHANAN: It seems to me your judgment that they have followed it involves the funny paradox that their doctrine is true.

MURRAY: I, if I am a good statesman, would try to lay down some basis for further expectations. I can find no other basis, in the first place. Secondly, I just think we have done ourselves in by meeting every concrete situation only when it arose in terms of a purely pragmatic response.

NIEBUHR: I would define pragmatism as a concession to historical contingency. I would say that we have not been pragmatic enough. We have not been pragmatic because from Roosevelt to Eisenhower we had a fixed doctrine of anti-imperialism. According to this, the Russians and we were anti-imperialist. This is really a fantastic bit of our doctrine. As a matter of fact, we are dealing not only with Soviet imperialism but with American imperialism. Ours is a very reluctant imperialism because we have the power to influence the destinies of many nations.

MURRAY: I agree that we have not been sufficiently pragmatic. Probably it shows itself in the instance that you noted—our anti-imperialism. We somehow feel that it is morally wrong for anybody to have political power over anybody else. It is as simple as that. Our anti-imperialism, so called, is based upon this completely irrational dogmatic feeling.

REDFIELD: I think that the validity of your analysis as to the Russian purpose—inflexible dynamism against the West— might be open to some criticism on the ground that you seem to be accepting that inevitable opposition between communism and the West which they also accept. If I may put it harshly, you sound just as Hegelian as they do.

*   *   *   *   *

KERR: I would agree with Father Murray's point that an understanding of the Communist ideology is absolutely basic to an understanding of Russian policy. One can't really understand what has happened within Russia without an understanding of this ideology, because if you look upon it just as leaders subject to political pressures they certainly would not have done what they have done. You cannot otherwise understand the tremendous emphasis on investment, the massive exploitation of the workers which has taken place—the greatest exploitation in the world today. If ideology is absolutely basic and if they do not respond to political pressures and ethical motives as we tend to in the West, then it is important to know where this ideology would lead them in the world scene. I would agree that logically it leads them to world domination, if (a) they continue their ideology, and (b) if it is possible for them to dominate the world physically.

But how do you oppose, if you wish to oppose, a nation with such an ideology so that it will not conquer the world and destroy what we consider to be basic values in human life? There are two ways of doing this. One would be to help them, to the extent we can, in the change of their ideology so that over time they do not remain what they now are; or, second, through direct opposition—just standing in front of them and saying you can go no further. Our dilemma is that these two methods work in opposite directions. If you want to change their ideology, you would say let us be nice to them, let us persuade them that they can live with capitalism, let us have a lot of exchange back and forth. Direct opposition means maintaining the solid front, building up armaments as they build up armaments, and so forth; to some extent reinforcing their current ideology that there has to be a war between the two worlds. What do you do when you are faced with this dilemma? My answer would be that the only thing you can do is to work for time. Two things are necessary to make the time constructive. You have to balance their power with your power. This means particularly at the scientific and military levels, but hopefully to balance their military power through disarmament agreements at the lowest possible level. At the same time, try to work to restructure the situation so that over time their ideology might be changed or the situation might be changed so you did not have to rely forever on this balance of power. So, then, how would you restructure the situation?

One, the reason you get peace in industrial relations despite all the strikes is that you very seldom see the destruction of one party by the other as you do in international relations. In industrial relations you have a situation really of mutual survival. If the union destroys the plant, it has destroyed the employment of its members. This is not quite as true on the other side. If the employer destroys the union, he has not destroyed to the same extent his work force. But he has destroyed, in the bitter battle which will take place, a good deal of the morale and the support he otherwise would have. How do you achieve this kind of mutual survival in international relations? I would say that the only answer to that, and it is not a full answer, is to trade. The more trade you can have back and forth, the greater dependence you have economically, as, for example, between Canada and the United States.

Second, in industrial relations you have two power organizations with the same citizenry; that is, the workers are the citizens of the plant. They are also the citizens of the trade union. As such they have a good deal of knowledge about both sides, and can exercise some influence. In international relations the closest you can get to that is by having the fullest possible cultural exchange, particularly at the intellectual level, appealing to the new intellectual elite in Russia. Any advance in industrial society becomes very dependent upon its intellectuals. Really the future, I am sure, belongs to the intellectually trained. You can get a little closer if people in both countries have about the same information and trade knowledge back and forth.

Three, in industrial relations the reason you get peace is that you have a superior external power which is the state, the community, with its rule of law. This would suggest working in the direction of a more powerful world rule of Law all the time. I would say at the same time that none of these things is anywhere near as easy to do in the international scene as it is in the domestic scene of industrial relations.

MURRAY: How do you sustain the necessary measure of implacability against a force that I would myself judge to be implacable without going over into a political policy of unconditional surrender, which I would consider to be just as disastrous as our military policy of unconditional surrender was? How do you do this balancing in the middle?

BURDICK: There is one point where the analogy falls down between the plant and the planet. On the planet level you each have as the hole card the potential to destroy the other. We can't do any of the things that you have indicated until we assure the first thing, which is time. This is why survival has become so important.

MURRAY: I don't have too much trouble with the notion of survival. The famous Russian sneak attack I think is nonsense. They are interested in the survival of the world revolution, and they will not do anything to imperil its course. The only purpose of my paper was to fill out the idea—yes, of course, co-existence but let us be quite clear in our own minds what we are called upon to co-exist with, or, if you want to speak of accommodation, let us be very clear what we are accommodating.

* * * * *

CHAIRMAN: Would Dr. Buchanan care to elaborate his proposition that because the Russian theory is false, therefore they cannot act in accordance with it?

BUCHANAN: There is very little of the Marxist-Leninist-Stalinist dogma being followed in any literal way at all. The thing has not panned out. It seems to me that externally there is a certain kind of childishness and irresponsibility about Russian foreign policy. It does not show the kind of solidity or substantiality that Father Murray is imputing to them. It does not seem to me they are being doctrinaire and wise in terms of their own ideology about their moves at all.

KERR: In what sense is it false? It is obviously an ideology which can be used to organize a modern industrial state and attain a great deal of economic progress within that state, as well as ability for the ideology and its proponents to survive over a period of time. In terms of survival value it certainly is not false. As I see it, the essence of the ideology is this: The technology must be absolutely supreme. That is the one real consideration. You must wipe away all aspects of the pre-existing culture which stand in the way of fulfilling the technological possibilities of the modern world. This technology can best be advanced through the mechanism of the state, through the power of the state, relying on a unified party, relying on a police force. Only through the power of the state can you wipe out the centers of opposition which might arise to the fulfillment of the technology—the church, independent trade unions, humanitarian considerations. Only through the power of the state can you exploit the people sufficiently to get the maximum amount of investment which allows the growth of scientific investigation and of capital goods to release the modern technology. The so-called withering away of the state I think you can put aside as a lot of chaff which was talked about to appeal to some intellectuals and draw them into the fold. It is an ideology which is trying to give modern technology its fullest scope, regardless of the cost, regardless of any other considerations.

NIEBUHR: It seems to me you left out one thing. The original Marxist theory was that property was the source of all injustice. You wipe out property and then you have by definition a just society and a non-imperialistic state. That is obviously false.

KERR: Sure it is false in that sense. I don't think myself that justice or injustice really has much to do with it. I would argue, and I think the facts prove it, that there is the most massive exploitation of the workers in Russia of any place in the world. In Western society about two-thirds of the national product goes to wage- and salary-earners. In Russia it is only about one-third.

CHAIRMAN: What is the appeal?

KERR: It is the ideology of forced draft industrialization. While we were getting industrialized a little over a century ago, and in England a century and a half ago, industry was something to be hated. Now today the revolution and the protest are not against industrialization in the capitalist form but in favor of industrialization in any form provided it is successful. That is what the Communists offer.

BUCHANAN: What relation does this have to the original Marxist-Leninist doctrine?

KERR: Not very much. This goes back in history before Marx, the idea that technology has to be freed.

CHAIRMAN: The only way you can sell this is on the theory, as Marx sold it, that nineteenth century capitalism is cruel and unjust. We want the benefits of industrialization; we do not want the cruelty and the injustice. The way we get this industrialization without cruelty and injustice is to have the state take it over.

KERR: I say that is just the sales talk.

CHAIRMAN: What we are trying to find out is what the ideology is.

KERR: I don't believe that has anything to do with it. I say you find a person's or system's ideology in what they do. The one thing they have always done is to free technology and the science which stands behind the technology. That is the one thing which goes the whole way through. I think that is the essential ideology. I would agree with Dr. Niebuhr's point that we need to have world areas under our influence through ideas and aid, and we better get the ideas and aid to them. I am all for that. Take a situation like that in Ghana where they want to make progress. They got their independence. They want to move ahead. How are they going to do it? They look to the United States and they see that we have an independent labor movement which fights the employers. But their trade union movement asks: Can we really fight the employers and hold up progress? Don't we have to ally ourselves with the state and push for economic progress instead of exercising a protest function? They are now looking very strongly to Israel and a movement which is not really like an American trade union movement at all, but a mechanism for the economic development of Israel. Ghana looks at the West and sees conflict. They say a rich society can afford conflict. We can't. We have to unify to move ahead. We can only unify along with the state. We don't want to go as far as Russia has gone, because that is too much exploitation and too little freedom and the trade union is merely an agent of the state. We have to find some place in between.

I think that was your point, Dr. Niebuhr, that we have to be more sympathetic to these alternatives and not condemn them because they are different from our pluralistic system with its regulated conflict. We have to find some ideas and start selling them to keep control over sufficient world areas, as well as enough military and scientific strength, to balance Russia during this interim period while we are trying to restructure the total situation.

*   *   *   *   *

BUCHANAN: I would like to ask Father Murray: Do you think Russia is working it out? Do you think that dialectical materialism is covering all of these phenomena?

MURRAY: The success in the long run is not the point. It may be the ethic of failure in the long run. That I have no trouble in accepting at all. You just can't do this kind of thing. The truth is on the reverse side of pragmatism—that whatever is not true will somewhere fail to work. This whole thing is going to fail to work.

NIEBUHR: You might say if we were lucky and were not going to be annihilated in this whole struggle, this might be subject to the same developments that came about in Anglo-Saxon history under the theory of royalism.

MURRAY: The only trouble I have with that is this: The thing we confront at the moment is unique. The imperialism here cannot survive except on the basis of the ideology and vice versa. The whole process of historical analogy, which is the only way we have of understanding what goes on, is something that I would be a little bit careful about. The old thing always was that the initial fanaticism was dulled either by success or by failure; it wouldn't matter which. This particular thing seems to be able to survive both so far and therefore has no historical parallel.

GOLDMAN: Father Murray, from this conception of yours relating to the uniqueness of the situation, it seems to me that a kind of grim determinism gets into your analysis. I wonder if it is not overly pessimistic and in some sense inaccurate. The question always is: What are we trying to co-exist with? Either your answer or Kerr's answer is overly simple and rather unhistorical. You say, as I understand it, that we are trying to deal with an inflexible dogma. Kerr says we are dealing with a doctrine of technological change. Could we not recognize that their stage at the present time is in part both of these, in part national interest, which Russia has been pursuing since long before communism, in part a kind of race war, in part a humanitarian drive? This situation is not unique in the world. It is confused, it is complex, it is like the French revolution. What is unique, it seems to me, is not the situation, but our reaction to it. In the past, when we have met such confused and complex world revolutionary situations, we have tended to be more adaptable. We have tended to be accommodatable. We are not now. The obvious reason we are not is that we have talked ourselves into believing that the things that are going on represent an attack on values we cannot change or adapt. There are certain bedrock values involved in this. This leads to the question whether this definition of the world situation necessarily forces us back on bedrock values and whether it is accurate.

KERR: May I follow up my view of the Russian scheme as being forced draft industrialization? I think, incidentally, that this forces some changes on them. I would feel that we ought to play for time until their internal contradictions catch up with them. The single-minded emphasis upon technology eventually is going to bring very great changes within Russia, and that is why we are fighting for time, until some of the changes take place. First, technology is basically dependent upon science. So you have to put a tremendous amount of money into education. Then you get the phenomenon of the intellectual elite being the most important group in your society. For the sake of advancing technology you have to have an advance in science, and that means these intellectuals have to keep up with the world and are developing more and more power all the time. You can't handle them as easily as you handle the managers. You cannot handle them as easily as the peasants and the military.

Additionally, I would like to point out that in the occupational hierarchy, as technology goes on, there arises a more and more diverse structure. Under this educated layer skilled groups will also get power and professional status. They will move around; you can't keep your hands on them. Second, the level of living over time also is bound to rise. As it rises, you get more people into the service trades, which do not lend themselves to as much central control. You get into more variation in food production, and can't run it like the production of wheat or the production of military equipment. As you get into diversification of products, you have to break down your industrial system into smaller units, and you have to give more authority to those units to adjust to all the little markets which spring up. All this will also bring greater leisure, and with greater leisure there will come more travel, more reading, a more educated mass generally. As a result of these factors the contradictions between the mass and the ruling class will build up and inevitably force changes within the system if we give it time and help it along.

MURRAY: So these changes take place. Could you make some educated conjecture as to the effect of this on foreign policy? These are domestic changes within the Russian complex as such. How will these changes, operating inside, affect foreign policy?

KERR: My guess is that they will soften the whole system both internally and externally over time.

MURRAY: Would you hold with those who say that the danger in foreign policy comes the moment the system is softened internally?

KERR: Yes. During the current period they are going through the softening-up process, while the ruling class is trying to hold on as the mass changes, and they may want to use external threats for the sake of maintaining ruling-class power. That is why you have to maintain your balance of power in the meantime so that they can't go wild with it for internal purposes.

NIEBUHR: About this danger point, wouldn't it be right to say that the danger point is when the ruling oligarchy gets desperate? Therefore, the policy must be not to confront them with an absolute fact.

KERR: Not make them desperate, but hope that it will change slowly enough so that they can adjust.

MURRAY: Somehow or other, I don't know how this is done, removing survival as a political or even military issue.

GOLDMAN: I am led to the question: Are we engaged in a life-and-death struggle involving fundamental values? It seems to me that Kerr's analysis still assumes this in the sense that we have the good values and what we should do is maneuver and wait and so forth and let them hang themselves. Is that correct?

KERR: Yes, I assume that we have the good values.

GOLDMAN: And that there are things in all of this which we cannot reconcile ourselves to without giving up our fundamental values?

KERR: Yes.

GOLDMAN: I would take the position that there is not anything very much that we cannot adjust to within the American tradition.

BUCHANAN: What we are looking for here is some way of co-existing with or tolerating socialist revolutions all over the world. They are of many forms, they are very inventive, and so on. They are not in themselves the new world. Socialism, it seems to me, as you look at it now, including the Russian form, is a receivership for bankrupt societies. It also is a step towards a kind of freedom and justice which these societies have not had. Our problem is to exist as a capitalist society in, possibly, a completely socialist revolutionary world. The purpose of socialism is to sort out the possible institutions in a kind of melting pot and to rearrange them into a form that we have not yet imagined; technology, of course, is the great power under this. The dynamism of it is fundamentally technological and scientific. I agree with Kerr on all that he was saying on that.

MURRAY: Do you think that communism is striving to do this thing, sorting out viable institutions?

BUCHANAN: Yes. I don't think they imagine their intention to be this except on occasion, but they show signs of doing it like mad. In very early stages they did.

*　　*　　*　　*　　*

BURDICK: I think you join the issue in a very direct way. What Goldman suggests is that Soviet communism is pluralistic. Kerr suggested that it will change. Father Murray says flatly that if it changes, the whole thing will collapse. Here I think is the central issue. They are committed to a material metaphysics. There is no question of that. There has been a high degree of consistency about it. But it seems to me that there is a considerable amount of evidence that they have changed the ideology a great deal. Can you give an example of what you think a failure to change in a basic issue has been?

MURRAY: If you ask the question with respect to decades or generations, I would maintain that the basic ideology, the atheism and materialism, would be entirely controlling. I would never undertake to explain any individual maneuver or tactic in terms of the ultimate atheism or materialism. I would take no such simple view as that. But in the long run this is the central thing. If they allowed free discussion among variants of the Communist line as it may have changed over the decades and generations of its existence, if some such basic change as this were to take place, then I would say that the structure is turning into something else. It may turn into something we can live with. That I don't deny. Therefore, I would welcome all such changes just as I would welcome the changes that Kerr has projected. But then that has nothing to do with policies that I have to adopt at the moment. When these changes have occurred, then I will begin my process of accommodation. Just at the moment I do not see that this is anything we can accommodate to.

CHAIRMAN: Couldn't we make the same mistake Marx made? Marx looked at nineteenth century capitalism and said this is the way it is always going to go.

KERR: Also there is in their basic theory the idea of thesis and antithesis. There must be some antithesis going on within the Russian system itself.

MURRAY: I agree. To that extent I am an Hegelian, too. What I am afraid of here is that we interpose between ourselves and the Russian reality a theory of freedom and contingency which underlies part of what I call the West. They don't. Their basic belief is deterministic.

MILLIS: You said, Father Murray, that after 1945 fellow-traveling governments controlled the new states, which they did not. The Russians were engaged in a battle as to whether Poland would be controlled essentially by the West or by the Communists. The origin of the cold war grew up not in a situation in which Russia was completely in control of things but when she was facing what seemed to her an attempt of the West to suppress her again, and brought back the memories she had of the post-1918 period and the Western intervention at that time. To say her actions were wholly stupid except as you explain them on the grounds of an ideology of world conquest is a misreading of history. To say that in the United States, Great Britain, and France a mood of good will prevailed that was pathological is an extraordinarily strong statement. While you might say that the general tone, especially of the more liberal American voices of opinion, was favorable to Russia, on the other hand there was very violent opposition to Russia within the United States. We had just fired the atomic bomb and showed ourselves in possession of a weapon which was regarded at that time as absolute. A lot of voices in the country were saying we have got the absolute weapon, let us put it up to the Russians and tell them to put up or shut up. That attitude was there. We got the Truman-Atlee statement, which implied an offer, in 1945. It was not until 1946, after Stalin's famous statement of February 15, which was widely regarded as the declaration of the cold war, that the Baruch Plan was put out. I have never regarded the Baruch Plan as something that could have looked to the people in the Kremlin as a genuine offer.

For some of the reasons I have just indicated, it does not seem to me that your analysis is an accurate depiction of what it is we are trying to co-exist with. When you put together Kerr's remarks and Goldman's and add them together, then perhaps you get a fairer picture of what we are trying to co-exist with, in which doctrine has some importance but is not controlling, and in which the necessity for industrialization has very great importance, but again is not wholly controlling, and so on. Regardless of when we have decided what it is we are co-existing with, I am puzzled as to what practical use we can make of this knowledge. You offer your analysis of what we are co-existing with but are unable to offer any suggestion or prediction, nor are you offering any suggestion as to how the action not predicted could be met.

MURRAY: There has been something new let loose. That is my basic intuition. I can only give it as an intuition. The basic thing I am trying to protest against is trying to understand this thing in the light of certain categories that we find familiar, that are congenial to our mentality and are based on our own experience and European experience in general. These I distrust. Why I wanted to emphasize the uniqueness of this thing is that if you overlook it, I think you are in bad trouble.

GOLDMAN: Do I understand that you would rule out any interpretation of what is going on in the world as simply a continuation in somewhat new forms of the ancient problem of tyranny?

MURRAY: Here I would have to reach for a fairly ultimate position. This, I think, is the first time you have had in history a tyranny—a political tyranny—formally and deliberately organized on the basis of atheism.

BUCHANAN: The ordinary voting machinery we are living with at present is not working very well anywhere. There is a kind of groping for a new kind of politics. We have to invent some new political forms to deal with these monster states, and the strange things that have happened to citizenship all over the world. Seventeenth century England was also threshing through a period in which some great inventions were made; at least we still think so. Couldn't this be happening right now?

MURRAY: I don't think so because all I can see is a variant of the manipulation of the masses by an elite. What is the relation between technology and politics? The Soviet Union has established one very definite, clearly defined relationship. We also have established a particular relationship. The other nations may be seeking one or another variant of either the American or the Soviet concept of the relationship. What they have in common in the world revolution is the simple thing of escape from misery. There is no reason under science and technology why people should be so miserable as they hitherto have been, why there should not be enough to eat, adequate shelter, reasonable comfort in life, and so on and so on. According to what political formula are the resources of science and technology to be utilized in order to effect this highly desirable result? That seems to me to be in a very broad statement pretty much the issue in conflict, or in doubt, at the moment.

NIEBUHR: There is another thing in the world revolution. It is not merely technology. It is national freedom against the infringement of European imperialism of the seventeenth to nineteenth centuries. That is a great part of the revolution.

MURRAY: Yes, but the question is whether they want national freedom as a means toward economic advancement or as an end in itself.

NIEBUHR: They might want both. The Indonesians are probably willing to sacrifice a good deal of economic efficiency for the sake of absolute freedom.

MURRAY: They are exploring, I suppose, the theoretical implications as well as the institutional implications of what is one of the phenomena of the world revolution, namely, that the old, eighteenth century, clear-cut distinction between politics and economics has completely disappeared. This we know better now. The era of laissez-faire liberalism and capitalism is simply outworn. You cannot separate and compartmentalize politics and economics. We worked it out over history in terms of various oscillations. They in turn are beginning to try to work it out. I don't know what the end result will be. I think I would still stick with my admittedly moral and intuitive judgment of condemnation of the Soviet system both in terms of its theory and also in terms of the casualties that have come forward in the course of its practice. Whatever else, not this, I would say.

BUCHANAN: You could do that with the stages of any revolution. The British Revolution in the seventeenth century or the French Revolution—you would want to condemn some of those steps, too. They were pretty awful, pretty immoral, pretty evil.

NIEBUHR: Could I suggest a possible consensus between you and the rest of us about the uniqueness of the Russian system? I at least would accept the fact that the consistency of the dogmatism and the pretension of the redemptive quality of the revolution are almost unique. Nevertheless, there is nothing unique in history that does not have some kind of a pattern. We find all kinds of patterns. The French Revolution we have obviously stated. If one can analyze what is unique and what is general in the patterns of history, I think we could reach some agreement and say there is a unique consistency in the Russians' dogmatism and there is a unique relationship of a power system to the dogmatism as there has never before been. It is also unique in the spread of its success. This does not change the fact that historical contingency can dilute any kind of dogma and may be diluting this dogma, or may be corrupting it or emptying it of dynamic meaning, without ever changing the symbols. History empties symbols of meaning, changes the dynamism. It seems to me that your excellent statement of uniqueness errs on the side of leaving out the pragmatism of history, the adjustment to the contingencies of history.

MURRAY: It has changed within itself—changed both in theory and also in practice. All I have been saying is that as of the moment no basic change has occurred, and, secondly, that when the basic change does occur it will be something quite other than it is now, and then we will be confronted with a situation quite other than what we are now confronted with. Our problem at the moment is not, however, to confront the thing that will be after the changes have occurred, but the thing that is now, which I believe is still acting according to its nature, a nature still essentially unaltered.

* * * * *

CHAIRMAN: Do we agree with the Kerr formula about the way in which this should be confronted, which I take to be a maintenance of what he called the balance of power?

KERR: What I say is that if during this stage in which they do confront us with an ideology which works towards world revolution we can hold them off through some balance of power, then the long-run trends of the world are working in such a direction that we don't have to keep the balance of power forever. We could have peace on some other basis. Father Murray's argument, as I understand it, would really mean that we had to have a balance of power forever because neither they nor we are going to change, or that if it was not possible to have a balance of power forever, then one side or the other would find it advantageous at some moment to break the peace and conquer the other side. We might choose our moment.

GOLDMAN: The success of your hypothesis depends on the prediction that by and large the forces which are at work will take the world toward certain values that we hold good.

KERR: I would say that eventually industrialization is going to bring a world-wide system. That is in its very nature. This world-wide system will be a pluralistic one, more nearly like our own than the monolithic system of Russia. This does not mean that every country is going to end up being exactly like every other country, but more like us than them. I think that is inherent in industrialization. I would argue—and I really do believe—that the industrial society is different in many ways from any type of society we have ever had in history. We cannot just generalize from the past. We have to take a new look at this new form of society. It will be more pervasive around the world than anything before. It will be more dynamic than anything we have ever had before. It will diversify people much more in their productive tasks than any society we have ever had before. It will bring a good many other differences. There is a logic in it which works in the direction of pluralism. Eventually, providing we can avoid catastrophe in the meantime, it will come out to be a pretty good society. I would say that men by and large in the long run adapt themselves pretty well.

MURRAY: But you would not exclude the possibility that it may also turn out the most destructive thing we ever had.

KERR: It could. I just don't think it is going to happen.

CHAIRMAN: Let us ask what the bearing of these remarks is on Father Murray's proposition which, I think, could stand some further explication in relation to the question of maximum risk and minimum security. We have just touched on that and I think it is a very important point to understand. As I understand your proposition, Kerr, you are not going to take any very great risks militarily, and that is not the way I understand Father Murray.

MURRAY: In the Hungarian affair, for example, I would rather have hoped that there would have been some people sitting in the State Department with nothing else to do except figure out what would be likely to happen in a place like Hungary or in the whole belt, if you will, of satellite states. I should have thought that somebody would have thought of the possibilities of an armed or semi-armed or almost unarmed revolt of the Hungarian type, and what we would do in such a case, and what the risks might be in doing them. What could we afford to do—ranging from nothing at all, which is what we did, through moral indignation, through what I call nicely calculated military intervention? I do not necessarily mean dropping paratroopers into Austria. We might have parachuted arms. It might have been simply a token intervention with arms as its symbol in some fashion, not necessarily troops stepping over the border. I don't know what it might have been. I am not a military expert.

MILLIS: To the extent that we could get a clearer idea of what the real restraints on the Russians are, that we could make a clearer evaluation of the risks involved in military or similar policy—no one could oppose that. I do have the idea that this is awfully difficult to do. Military factors are just not susceptible to that kind of reasonable rational analysis. Most people are apt to think they are. But you never know what you are going to get when you resort to force. You never can firmly decide how the results are going to fall out.

NIEBUHR: We have left out of our recent conversations what was very much on our minds months ago. That was the new dimension arising out of the common predicament between us and the Russians, which does not cancel out any of the differences we have but makes all the analogies of history

115

faulty, because no competing empires have ever had the situation before that they would destroy themselves as they destroyed each other.

MURRAY: I am substantially attacking the problem on the level of understanding, which indeed was the level that I think Millis was operating on.   How do you understand the situation that confronts us?   Millis understood it in one way. I tried to understand it in other terms and on a different level.   This is all right.   This is a contribution to public understanding.

FUND FOR THE REPUBLIC PAMPHLETS

Individual Freedom and the Common Defense
by Walter Millis

Economic Power and the Free Society
by A. A. Berle, Jr.

Unions and Union Leaders of Their Own Choosing
by Clark Kerr

The Corporation and the Republic
by Scott Buchanan

Religion and the Free Society
by William Lee Miller, William Clancy, Arthur Cohen,
Mark DeWolfe Howe, and Maximilian W. Kempner

Single copies available free from the Fund
60 East 42nd Street, New York 17, N. Y.
Prices on bulk orders provided on request.